£5.   n188

IN THE FOOTSTEPS OF
LAWRENCE OF ARABIA

IN THE FOOTSTEPS OF
LAWRENCE
OF ARABIA

CHARLES BLACKMORE

Harrap . London

Produced by PILOT PRODUCTIONS LIMITED
59 Charlotte Street, London W1P 1LA

First published in Great Britain 1986
by HARRAP LIMITED
19-23 Ludgate Hill, London EC4M 7PD

Photoset by Communitype in Leicester
Printed by Mandarin in Hong Kong

The author and publishers would like to thank the
following for supplying their photographs for
inclusion in this book: Rothmans International,
Radio Times Hulton Picture Library, Bill Lyons, and
Jefferson Price III.

Expeditions rely upon the goodwill of numerous individuals and organisations. In particular I wish to thank the following for their generosity in providing financial and material support: Rothmans International, British Airways, Survival Aids, Survey and General Instrument, Standard Life Insurance, Casio Electronics, The School of Military Survey, and Whipsnade Zoo. To the following I owe special thanks: the Jordanian Armed Forces, and in particular Brigadier Shobaky, Colonel and Mrs David Whitten, the British Embassy in Amman, Mr H St J B Armitage CBE, Colonel (Retd) T N Bromage OBE, and Karen Sheldrake for her typing. I am extremely grateful to Tom Beaumont for the hours we have spent together and for re-living his recollections of T E Lawrence during the Arab Revolt. My warmest thanks to my wife, Tina, for her endless support and advice during the drafting of chapters for this book. Also I am very grateful to the many other helpers, both family and friends, whose names I have not the space to record. Finally to Piers Dudgeon who made this book possible. A special token of my respect is extended to Mohammed Musa and Hamad Awad of the Howeitat in Wadi Rumm, Jordan - to have shared so much with them was a privilege and an everlasting memory.

CDB
Hong Kong
April, 1986

Contents

Foreword

At my school in Suffolk the oak-panelled library was lined with the most wonderful collection of books. I can remember exploring this labyrinth one afternoon at the age of eight, and have a vivid memory of picking from the shelf a copy of *Seven Pillars of Wisdom*. Quite why it was this particular book I cannot be certain. I know the title attracted my attention but I suspect at that age it was something more fundamental. It may have been the crossed Arabian swords on the cover which reminded me of the kukri motif of the Gurkhas with which I was so familiar (my father was serving with them in Singapore where I too had lived the previous four years). Of course I didn't read the book, either then or for many years until I was mature enough to understand the challenging complexity of Lawrence's writing. Nevertheless I did develop an early interest in Lawrence's part in the Arab Revolt. In this I was unwittingly helped by my grandfather, who had served throughout the First World War in the Middle East. Later he was with General Allenby when Jerusalem and Damascus were captured - Lawrence and the Arab Army supported both operations by attacking the lines of communication and flanks of the Turks. The stories of those years, the albums of faded photographs, and above all the books and press cuttings of Lawrence, all rubbed off on me during childhood visits to my grandfather's Suffolk farmhouse near my school. Later, in my teens, I spent hours diligently re-doing his scrapbooks of the campaign in Palestine, and through this began to understand his love for the country and his respect for Lawrence.

The enigmatic legend surrounding Lawrence of Arabia makes him one of the most documented and controversial figures in recent history. It appeals to every dreamer and romantic, no less to me as I travelled through Jordan and Israel in my early twenties. And no doubt my feelings were enhanced by a love of history. I was not a hero-worshipper in the strict sense, otherwise I would have been blind to Lawrence's shortcomings. Nevertheless my fascination with the man developed at a time when I lacked direction in my life, and his qualities focused my attention on what would be required of me if I was to become note-worthy.

My impressions of Lawrence were intensified by a visit to the Middle East in 1981. I returned and read *Seven Pillars of Wisdom* properly, only then (because I had witnessed the context in which his story occurred), understanding the author's play of words. With further reading I became aware of the true extent of his life after the First World War, and in discovering this entered a new phase: I was more searching and analytical, my mind stimulated by biographers seeking to interpret the meaning of his life and often trying to shine light on some hitherto dark secret. This interpretive approach served to alter and even tarnish my image of the man, although I remained in no doubt of his achievements and importance when I arrived in Jordan to begin the expedition.

The expedition was not in answer to a lifetime's ambition; it grew from my interest in Lawrence and the need to find more challenge and variety than the Army could offer at that moment. Never was there even the remotest intention to write a book, since I felt that anyone writing about Lawrence risks traversing a minefield of controversy and criticism. Too many people have stepped on the Lawrence bandwagon to exploit the sizable clientele of admirers and sceptics. I certainly did not wish to join them. By chance an offer did come to write about my Jordanian journey and, because it was a story of the desert and the Bedouin, I felt that I should try.

I have written nothing new or sweeping about Lawrence; I have striven to write my thoughts and feelings as they occurred each day. The account is based entirely on my diaries and in certain instances they are quoted, word for word. Its substance is a traveller's tale, and therein lies its true value.

Living so closely to the land and people of *Seven Pillars*, we were bound to form our own impressions - sometimes unexpected - but these were the result of thoughts and conversations that occurred on a particular day and in circumstances peculiar to that day, or they occurred in response to a gradual awareness of the relevance of passages in Lawrence's book to our situation. My account of such impressions is faithful to the circumstances in which they occurred and, consequently, may give rise to some inconsistencies which I have not sought to change. For the same reason I do not attempt to summarise my feelings about Lawrence as the chapters unfold. What I have tried to do is to bring the reader into the expedition as it happened, as a member of the party, able to make his own observations and deductions.

Our aim was not to prove or disprove anything about Lawrence. We sought merely to trace 1,000 miles of his journeys, charting our route by the maps and descriptions in *Seven Pillars of Wisdom*. It was a commemorative venture to coincide with the fiftieth anniversary of his death, and to make our interpretation more authentic we chose to adopt the dress and ways of the Bedouin handlers of the Howeitat tribe who accompanied us. Neither we nor they felt us unworthy of this. Alone, in the vastness of the desert, it was the natural thing to do. Only when we reached the more inhabited parts of Jordan in the last week of the ride did we become at all self-conscious: at times thinking our clothes to be a sham, an inappropriate disguise, and at others relishing our concealment and dissimilarity to the orthodox tourist.

At the outset we were ill-prepared for, and naive about, the severe contrast between our ways and those of the Bedouin: initially, we had no knowledge of Arabic and - more significantly - no knowledge of the Arab mind. This brought us into repeated conflict with the camel handlers, and threatened our success. But, in the end, our gradual education served both to broaden our outlook and contribute to the colour and excitement of the journey. Learning about the Bedouin and their ways became a healthy alternative to disappointments regarding the history of Lawrence and the Arab Revolt.

Unintentionally, our interaction with the Bedouin, the camels and the desert began to eclipse our aim to search for the past by re-enactment alone. And here existed a further inconsistency: although we merged as far as possible with the traditions of desert tribesmen, and jealously guarded their ways, we soon realised that the encroachment of technology and 'civilisation' on their way of life was inescapable. We became confused in our identity - one week living the time-worn way of the Bedouin, and the next, standing with our camels in a modern town of tarmac roads and motor vehicles. I realised that the past could not be literally re-created, but I was totally caught up with the ethos of the earlier time. I transcribed my dilemma in diary form, and it is reproduced here, in book form, without all the loose ends having been tied together.

The expedition suffered many set-backs, frustrations and changes of plan, and at an early stage it became apparent that we would not achieve the intended 1,000 miles. Perhaps, in ignoring the advice of famous desert travellers, I had been over-ambitious. But the source of my reasoning had lain in *Seven Pillars of Wisdom*, where Lawrence wrote: 'In the last four weeks I had ridden fourteen hundred miles by camel, not sparing myself anything to advance the war.' My 1,000 miles seemed a credible goal, but I had ignored what I later came to call the 'x' factors: the poor fitness of modern-day camels no longer used to such demands, and Bedouin incapable of adjusting the leisurely routine of their existence to a tough expedition schedule. I was surprised that their endurance was not as strong as ours, and that it was they who asked to slow the pace or call for halts. The problem was that they did not share our motive for the venture.

But what kept us going in spite of this was an unexpected reward - the privilege and beauty of our co-existence with the Bedu. This was our most priceless and treasured gift. As Wilfred Thesiger wrote in *Arabian Sands*, 'No man can live this life and emerge unchanged. He will carry, however faint, the imprint of the desert, the brand which marks the nomad; and he will have the yearning to return, weak or insistent according to his nature. For this cruel land can cast a spell which no temperate clime can match.'

Introduction

'It was his eyes....these piercing blue eyes which seemed to look right through you that I shall always remember,' said Tom Beaumont, seated directly opposite me in the dining room of his house, El Aurens. Despite the warmth of the January sun that fills the room, the gas heater is on full, and the old soldier wears a thick dressing gown, neck cravat, socks and slippers. Tom Beaumont is in his late eighties and is frail after being laid low by a severe attack of shingles.

For four hours Tom reminisced about the desert and the Arab revolt; stories of putting down overhead fire with the machine gun as Lawrence blew up Turkish troop trains, more personal recollections of Lawrence's dress and conversation, and the particular hold he had over the Bedouin and his English soldiers.

Photographs of Lawrence lie about the floor, some well known but others rarely seen. Among them there is one that utterly captures my imagination. The picture was taken by Sir Ronald Storrs (a close friend after they had worked together in the Middle East) on 21 May, 1935, the day Lawrence was buried at Moreton Church in Dorset. I remember reading how Storrs had climbed a trestle to stand astride the coffin and take a timed exposure. He was interrupted half way through by the Coroner who had come to view the body. Nevertheless he had succeeded in taking six photographs, of which this one had come out reasonably well.

I shiver involuntarily. Storrs wrote later, 'Beyond a few small scars and a little discolouration of the left eye and region, Lawrence was looking handsomer and nobler than I had ever seen him. The nose sharp as a pen and more hooked and hawklike than in life and the chin less square...he was wrapped in white cotton wool with a tight bandage around the forehead and looser sheeting around him. He was, with almost no imagination, once more the Arab Chieftain in kaffiyah and aigal lying in

dark stained ivory against the dead white of the hospital stuff.'

I hold the photograph by the edges, almost afraid to move it. I feel as though a secret is being unfolded. The eyes of the dead man are closed and slightly swollen, and the prominent nose casts a fine shadow over his right cheek. The lips are delicately formed, almost sensuous and faintly feminine, they too are swollen. The square, proud jaw is grazed, the only discernable mark. A bandage across the forehead masks much of the damage. The face has shut its eyes on life and the physical being, a last wish before the coffin was sealed and the body entombed in the ground. But today remains the spirit and the controversy.

Tom shifts his position gingerly, his age showing in every movement. He has a wiry build and his short cropped hair emphasises his large ears. His face is lined and the skin below his chin has lost the tightness of youth. But Tom still displays an agile mind which is reflected in his small, intent eyes. I study him carefully, trying to see him as a youth. Tom is the only surviving Englishman actually to have fought alongside Lawrence of Arabia in the desert and been part of his irregular army of Arabs. There are obviously a few men still alive who met Lawrence in the First World War, but Tom is the only survivor mentioned in the Nominal Role in *Seven Pillars of Wisdom*. Helen his wife sits beside him and as well as providing the sandwiches, mince pies and beer, she has jogged his memory a few times, putting him back on the track of stories I most wanted to hear.

'El Aurens the Arabs called him...know what that means? It means "The Lawrence" because to them there could be only one. I expect you'll find that some remember him still by that name. How about salt, taking enough are you?...We used to have ruddy big tablets like horse pills to take every day.' I smile as he tut-tuts and nods his head at the memory.

Tom Beaumont, facing camera, squatting behind a Vickers Machine Gun in 1916.

'This was Tom aged nineteen,' says Helen, as she hands across a faded photograph before settling proudly back into her seat. 'Taken in Cairo, it was, before I joined Lawrence,' Tom explains. 'I was in the Machine Gun Corps...Vickers they was...expect you don't use them any more - marvellous guns, but water cooled. One day my officer had me in and asked whether I wanted to help train the Arabs up a bit with the Vickers...next day I was off. Going to Aqaba are you?' I tell him we are. 'I remember arriving there by boat: couldn't get near the shore and so the Navy boys ferried all our equipment and ourselves in small rafts...still had to wade to the beach mind. That's where I first met Lawrence...wasn't long after he and the Arabs had captured the town. He wrote to me you know.'

Helen interrupts at this point to say that all the letters and memorabilia are now in America, Tom had to sell them when he was hard up. I ask when he last saw Lawrence. 'October 1918, in Damascus,' he replies quietly. 'It was just after the city's capture and before Lawrence went back to England. In his letter to me in 1935, written two weeks before his fated accident, he wrote saying he promised to come and see me at my home in Yorkshire....but he was never to come.' Tom's voice trails off, and I can see that even in 1985 there is still regret.

PR and Planning

The day of the expedition press conference in the camel enclosure of Whipsnade Zoo, thirty-six hours before flying to the desert, the snow fell steadily as we stood facing a lone photographer from the Associated Press.

Images of the desert and Lawrence formed in the public imagination by *Beau Geste* and Peter O'Toole in David Lean's film were not to be found here. Dressed in scanty desert fatigues hastily purchased the same day from a London government surplus store, we felt utterly incongruous stamping our sandalled feet while blowing on our hands for warmth. A small but enthusiastic gathering of onlookers, more suitably dressed for the February weather, watched in safety from behind the iron railings. The approaching camels acted as a backdrop to the snowy picture. It was not an occasion filled with glory and fame, popping flashbulbs and pressmen eager for a Lawrence of Arabia story. We would have felt less ridiculous were it not for the white tea towels from the zoo canteen tied about our heads as kaffiyahs.

The reluctant camels were encouraged across the enclosure by their keeper with a bag of meal. He explained that it was their mating season which made them frisky. The camels snapped at each other, bucked and scrummed for priority in feeding. The first sight of such large and apparently uncontrollable animals did not fill us with confidence. I stood shivering in the snow with a camel nuzzling my back, knowing for certain that few papers would run our story the following morning.

Two hours later, with the feeling we were

Far left: *the author,* **Captain Charles Blackmore, 27.** *'The way we'd started off was very different to the way we ended up...going through pain but also finishing, then looking back, knowing yourself, having tested yourself, pitted yourself against the elements.'*

Left: **Bandsman Christopher Selley, 22.** *'Chris developed in a way known to himself alone.'*

embarking on something important, the expedition party had its final briefing in a cafe on the Luton to London road. I outlined the plan to ride 1,000 miles by camel across the Jordanian desert in order to retrace some of the journeys of Lawrence of Arabia. These he had ridden during the course of the Arab Revolt in the First World War, and the expedition aimed to follow a combination of the trails which he mapped and described in *Seven Pillars of Wisdom*. The timing of the event was to coincide with the 50th anniversary of his untimely death. It was to be a commemorative journey as well as being the first of its kind to follow Lawrence in a realistic fashion.

As I went through the final details I realised how poorly prepared we were. No one had an inkling of what to expect or any experience to meet it. Around the formica table, laden with coffee and hamburgers, were Captain James Bowden, Rifleman Mark West and Bandsman Chris Selley, and the only obvious qualification we shared was that of being serving soldiers in the Royal Green Jackets. They listened attentively as I spoke confidently with an impressively fat looking planning file beside me (mostly filled with 'we regret' letters from potential sponsors).

My own confidence was partially based on a brief attachment to the Jordanian army some years previously, but mainly from reading many books by desert travellers whose achievements, in their first chapters, far surpassed my

overall plan. James Bowden's role in the forthcoming venture was rather grandiosely titled Expedition Navigation Officer, a recent qualification after a last minute and very condensed astro-navigation course.

I first met James in Cyprus with the 3rd Battalion in 1980. A tall, old Etonian, he exudes all the positive qualities of an individual with slightly eccentric tastes. At twenty-five, he is single-minded with a refreshingly broad wit and intellect, characteristics all deceptively bundled into a loose and languid body which he carries around almost as an afterthought. He proved his worth on a similar commemorative expedition a year before, and I know him to be an ideal traveller.

Mark West and Chris Selley I barely know. The original plan was to incorporate a doctor and an Arab linguist into the team: after eight months of searching there were no such men freely available within the army.

Thus was the decision made, somewhat late, to take two private soldiers, who would not under normal circumstances be in a position to participate in such a venture. Mark was serving in the 2nd Battalion in Germany when, in response to my call for volunteers, we arranged to meet. The night before interviewing him I had read that the one essential criterion for selecting members of an expedition is to follow your gut feeling. I applied this to the polite twenty-two-year-old rather stocky character and with keen, honest answers, a hint of

Far right: **Rifleman Mark West, 22.** *'James had remarked once that if he had to picture a Brummy lad in the desert, then Mark was what he would expect.'*

Right: **Captain James Bowden, 25.** *'Only James could think of Napoleon's piles at 6 am in the morning.'*

humour and a straight-forward Birmingham manner, he met that criterion.

Chris Selley was recommended because he practised a strange form of Japanese martial art and slept on the floor. Neither were obviously significant qualifications for spending more than a month on camel back, but at least they suggested he was different. Aged twenty-two he had fair hair and very blue eyes. With his slight, athletic build and fresh complexion it was obvious the Arabs would associate him with stories of Lawrence. Quiet and self-conscious, a certain lack of confidence might well have been due to being blown up by the IRA in the Regents Park bombing of the 1st Battalion band two years previously. He was medically trained, since a bandsman's wartime role is that of a stretcher bearer in the Battalion. Following Chris' interview he was appointed to the position of Expedition Medic.The briefing finished, the party split up to Gloucester, Birmingham, Surrey and Dorset for their remaining day in England. I drove south with the accumulated tiredness of eight months of tenacious campaigning to make a small dream come true. Lawrence had written once, 'All men dream: but not equally. Those who dream by night in the dusty recesses of their minds wake in the day to find that it was vanity: but the dreamers of the day are dangerous men, for they may act their dreams with open eyes, to make it possible.'

The planning stage had been typical of any

expedition as nothing came together until the last moment. There had been many occasions while driving to work through the forest in Sennelager, Germany, optimistically repeating the *Teach Yourself Arabic* tape, when the temptation to wake had been strong. The original plan had been to ride over 1,500 miles through Saudi Arabia and Jordan. A departure date was fixed for 25 January. By the New Year there had been no official reply from Saudi despite the assistance of two London Arabists, Mr St John Armitage, CBE, and Colonel Nigel Bromage, CBE, who had been lobbying contacts as high as the Saudi Royal Family. Jordan would not commit itself until Saudi would. Over £12,000 was required to finance the expedition and £10,000 of that remained outstanding.

Without political clearance the sponsors were doubtful, and without sponsors it was difficult to make preparations for camels, handlers, supplies and contacts in both countries. Small booklets with sand coloured covers, including maps and flowing descriptions of the challenges ahead had failed to arouse interest. In a last minute attempt to salvage the expedition, the plan was changed to complete the entire 1,000 mile journey in Jordan. An agonising pause followed during which time James attended his navigation course and a fresh search was made for sponsors. The Defence Attaché in Amman, Colonel David Whitten cabled with contagious optimism. 'What is your exact route and dates? We can arrange camels to be purchased around

Aqaba.' With a new departure date of 10 February and a completely new plan, two remarkable successes in the final week guaranteed at least the expedition's arrival in Amman. First, British Airways were won over by James' eloquent charm and agreed to provide free flights in Club Class, and second, Rothmans International plc, generously offered £7,000: I had to ask them to repeat the offer at least three times before I could accept what I was hearing.

T E L

At the beginning of the First World War, Thomas Edward Lawrence was nearly twenty-six. During his university travels through countries now known as Syria, Israel, Jordan and the Lebanon, he built up an extensive knowledge of Arab people and the language. His passion was history. After leaving Jesus College, Oxford, he spent many months assisting Leonard (later Sir Leonard) Woolley in excavating an archaeological site at Carchemish in northern Syria.

Recent biographies have shown that Lawrence had begun his dual life even then, and that he was collecting information on the Middle East for his Oxford tutor, Dr D G Hogarth, an academic known to be connected with British Intelligence and interests in the area.

For the first two years of the war Lawrence worked in the Military Intelligence Department in Cairo. Using his extensive knowledge, and while manning a small network of spies, he compiled maps and prepared briefs on the distribution of Turkish forces in the Ottoman Empire, which had by then sided with the Germans. Meanwhile in France, two of his brothers were killed in action, and it has been suggested the effects of this made Lawrence seek a more active role in the war.

At the outbreak of war, the Ottoman Empire extended to Syria, Israel, Jordan, Iran, and Saudi Arabia. In order to ensure a consolidated victory against the Turks in the Middle East, it was in British interests to arouse and support Arab national sentiments to rebel against their Turkish overlords. By a combination of chance and careful manipulation, it was to be the Great Arab Revolt of 1916, initiated by Sherif Hussein in Mecca, to which Lawrence was devoted in the last two years of the war. He was to return a hero, 'the Champion of the Arabs', 'the Uncrowned King of Arabia' and 'the Prince of Mecca'.

The enduring legend began and was fuelled by public craving for romance, an enigmatic individual. Captain T E Lawrence, as yet without any formal military training, apart from his days in the Oxford University Officer Training Corps, appreciated the full significance and worth of an irregular army of Arabs, fighting to the flanks of the British regular forces in the drive north from Egypt to Damascus. He became a great exponent of the strategy.

It was not until October, 1916, that Lawrence was to become more closely involved in the Revolt. Ronald Storrs, then Oriental Secretary to the British Agency in Egypt, and an official held in high trust by the Arabs, went to Jedda to see what could be done to assist the flagging Revolt. His travelling companion was to be a 5 foot 5 1/2 inch, fair-haired, blue-eyed Captain from GHQ in Cairo.

Lawrence quickly impressed the Sherif's second son, Abdulla, with his perception and knowledge of the Arab cause and its associated problems. He arranged that Lawrence would ride inland to meet his brother Feisal, a man quickly assessed to be the one plausible leader of a prolonged and successful Revolt. Lawrence wrote later of that meeting, 'I felt at first glance that this was the man I had come to Arabia to seek - the leader who would bring the Arab Revolt to full glory.'

The capture of Damascus in October, 1918, ended over four hundred years of Ottoman rule in the Middle East. It also ended Lawrence's active role in the Revolt. For two years he had acted as political adviser to Feisal; he had been the instrument through which the British with their gold, military hardware, and paper promises of Arab independence and unity, had successfully used the Revolt to consolidate the victory of their regular forces. It was a betrayal which affected Lawrence deeply:

'I could see that if we won the war the promises to the Arabs were dead paper. Had I been an honourable adviser I would have sent my men home, and not let them risk their lives for such stuff. So I assured them that England kept her word in letter and spirit. In this comfort they performed their fine things: but, of course, instead of being proud of what we did together, I was continually and bitterly ashamed.'

Lawrence ended the war with the rank of Colonel. He was awarded the CB (Companion of the Bath) and DSO (Distinguished Sevice Order) for his part in a number of actions against the Turks. He declined both awards at a private investiture with King George V. Lawrence felt that His Majesty's government had broken pledges to Feisal which had been given in the King's name. The story became part of the enduring legend.

For two years Lawrence lived and dressed as an Arab, endured great hardship and assumed a responsibility which resulted in him being the principle focus of the Revolt. He led raids by camel against the Hejaz railway behind enemy lines and blew up a number of Turkish trains: the railway was the strategic and logistical link on which the success of the Revolt became virtually dependant; without it, the Turkish garrisons were isolated and vulnerable to attack from the army of irregular Bedouin. This strategy worked. It was the post-war Lawrence which stimulated so much of the controversy and legend which survives today, at its very least, as a household name. Someone will arrive at a fancy-dress party in Arabic costume to be greeted by, 'Who do you think you are, blinking Lawrence of Arabia?' Many such jests are based upon little knowledge of the real man, but the name and legend survive.

The American journalist, Lowell Thomas, helped ensure, albeit unintentionally, that Lawrence remained an international figure and one of the most unlikely heroes of the century. Thomas had been asked to find a story which would stimulate flagging public support for the protracted and bloody war. He found nothing in France. By chance, his encounter with the young fair-haired Englishman, and Oxford graduate, dressed in the flowing white robes of a Sherifan prince, who led the Bedouin into battle by camel, interested the Anglophile Thomas.

He had found his subject and he exploited it to the full. Reality was substituted by romance and exaggeration, and Thomas' post-war lecture tours credited Lawrence with everything and adorned him with an international reputation. Lawrence rose to it initially, as it fulfilled his secret youthful ambitions, but finally he backed away from the limelight.

Lawrence's immediate concern, following the capture of Damascus, was to ensure a fair settlement for the Arabs. To this end he was prominent as an adviser to Feisal at the Paris and Cairo Peace Conferences which finalised the victors' division of spoils. In a state of virtual mental breakdown and frustration with the political deceit, he left his new position in the Colonial Office in 1922. In August of the same year, an Aircraftman Ross joined the RAF and passed his medical entrance aged thirty-four. He was in poor health following his trials in the desert, yet he was granted this strange request to enter the ranks anonymously under the watchful eye and through the friendly influence of the Chief of the Royal Air Force, Trenchard.

In January, 1923, Aircraftman Ross alias 'Colonel T E Lawrence, CB, DSO, Croix de Guerre, Fellow of Jesus College Oxford, Uncrowned King of Arabia and Prince of Mecca' (*Who's Who*, 1923) was discharged from the RAF. He had irritated not only his senior officers, but his secret had been discovered and his cover blown by the press much to Trenchard's embarrassment.

Nevertheless Lawrence persisted in his search for anonymity in the ranks of the Services. After changing his name to Shaw, he arrived at the Royal Tank Corps Depot at Bovington, Dorset, on 12 March, 1923. Again it was by virtue of Lawrence's influential contacts that entry was permitted. While serving at Bovington, he found and rented the Cottage of Clouds Hill one mile north of the camp. It remains today as a National Trust Property, and it is marked on the *Reader's Digest* AA map as Lawrence of Arabia's home. In a recent biography of Lawrence, Michael Yardley claims that this insistence on serving in the ranks was rooted in his hope 'that the radical change to his life-style might bring to an end his agonizing confusion. He was still in search of an

Lawrence's grave at Moreton Cemetry. The headstone was a later addition and significantly refers to him as T E Lawrence rather than T E Shaw, his assumed name. 'There was a craving to be famous; and a horror of being known to like being known.' Seven Pillars of Wisdom

identity, he desperately wanted to belong, and he had been attracted for some time to the idea of service in the ranks. It was, as he himself noted, the modern alternative to a monastery. It offered a means of escape - escape from responsibility, from women and from the Frankenstein monster of his own fame. He looked forward to the discipline, the tightness of life, as a means to regenerate himself. He told Robert Graves that he wanted to become ordinary, to put himself on a common level with other men. The RAF would offer him a chance of a "brain-sleep". He predicted he would come out less "odd" than he went in.' Above all it gave him the security to write, and those early post-war years were to be spent absorbed in drafting *Seven Pillars of Wisdom*.

Trooper Shaw became intensely unhappy as a private soldier in the squalor of the Royal Tank Corps. In 1925 he successfully campaigned to rejoin the RAF, and on 24 August he reported for recruit training at Cranwell. Lawrence remained in the RAF for a further ten years, a time in his life during which he found semi-contentment with himself. He lived an extraordinary dual existence, remaining an Aircraftman but maintaining close friendships with George Bernard Shaw, Winston Churchill, Augustus John, Lady Astor and many other notable people in society. His influence was far reaching, and despite not wishing to hold power after 1918, his presence and personal charisma ensured he remained a popular myth despite many personal failings.

T E Lawrence died as a result of head injuries sustained in a motorcycle accident on the quiet country lane to Bovington camp near his cottage, Clouds Hill. To the shocked public at the time it became unbelievable that such an enigmatic and controversial hero could die in such a 'normal' way. Many theories, including a popular one of murder, have been advanced to solve the 'unacceptable' facts of his death. The official cause was congestion of the lungs and heart following a fracture of the skull and laceration of the brain.

Two and a half months after his death *Seven Pillars of Wisdom* was published. During his lifetime Lawrence had printed privately a limited number of copies but he had stipulated that only after his death could the work go on general release. In the introductory chapter, Lawrence clearly pointed out that the book was not a history of the Revolt but a narrative of his daily life in it. 'It is filled with trivial things, partly that no one mistake for history the bones from which some day a man may make history, and partly for the pleasure it gave me to recall the fellowship of the revolt. We were fond together, because of the sweep of the open places, the taste of wide winds, the sunlight, and the hopes in which we worked.' Under the title Lawrence wrote two simple words, 'A Triumph'.

The Expedition

In the journey south from Amman to the Red Sea port of Aqaba, the Wadi Araba is the geographical divide between the Dead Sea and the Red Sea. The military road leaves the main King's Highway at Karak and drops to the level of the Dead Sea at its southernmost end, there following the border south.

The afternoon air was hot and still in the Wadi Araba on 11 February, 1985. To the east a line of jebel paralleled the south bound border road; to the west, across an open desert with the contours of a dried out lake, lay Israel. The thin wire fence demarcating the border was a few hundred metres from the road and re-emphasised by the incised tracks of patrolling army vehicles. The white embassy landrover with CD plates, parked on the sandy verge where it had halted, out of fuel. Telling us that God had willed it, the Jordanian driver hitched a lift and returned with less than a jerry can of petrol three hours later. James passed the time teaching the others how to use the theodolite to take sun shots in the direction of Israel. Fortunately there was no reaction on the border to such a potentially dangerous blunder.

Forty miles on, the landrover coughed to its second halt, just beside a Jordanian army border position dug into the hillside. Again it had run out of petrol just as God had willed. Those of us able to raise a smile on the first day of acclimatisation, stranded somewhere between the Dead Sea and Aqaba, shared the feeling that at least the camels would not have such mechanical shortcomings. Things could only improve, which they did when Aqaba was finally reached later that night.

The four of us took a small room with two double beds in the Holiday Inn. The problems of living together became immediately and humorously apparent. I snored all night, and James fought with the bedclothes. The following morning, the second in Jordan, an Arabic breakfast was ordered. It was barely touched. Early days, but I was slightly disturbed by the apparent insularity of our way of life. I reminded them all that when they were starving in the desert they would give their right hand for such a meal.

'Yes, but right now we are not in the desert and we are not starving,' was Mark's practical rejoinder.

Outside, the sky was a deep blue and already the sea looked cool and inviting. Compared to the snow in England of thirty-six hours ago it was an exciting contrast.

One hour later I sat in the office of the Commander of the Southern Military Area of Jordan. Beside me was the Defence Attaché who had come to Aqaba to assist in the initial liaison with the Jordanians. Both he and his wife Rosemary had been charming and enthusiastic towards us four future cameliers who had no

13 February. *The team loads up the landrover at Aqaba before heading for Wadi Rumm.*

'After getting food and our thobes I said, "Let's start now", and Mohammed said, "Fine," and we went in an army landrover wearing our government surplus desert uniform as if going on safari.'

real idea of what was in store. Rosemary's affinity stemmed from her own unorthodox journey with a donkey and trap from Cornwall to London one summer. The Jordanian Brigadier was a small man with an engaging smile; more important, he looked helpful. I sat looking at the pictures of the dashing King Hussein beside his more sober looking brother, the Crown Prince.

Outside, the hills of Aqaba were a ruddy red against the sky. Small and delicately coloured humming birds hovered near the window over the minute stamens of a freesia, and became the subject of conversation for some minutes. Finally, after a private soldier had brought small cups of bitter coffee, the day's business began.

'Now, what can I do to help?' the Brigadier asked in good English. His manner suggested he had planned nothing; clearly we were starting from scratch.

I knew how important the meeting was. We were in Aqaba with the equipment and money, but without the clearance to move freely, and without the co-operation of the native Bedouin for camels and handlers, the expedition could not get underway. So, I outlined our needs for six camels and a reliable handler to cover 1,000 miles in one month. The Brigadier's face remained impassive and attentive. I explained the route and the purpose of the expedition,

steering away from the Lawrence aspect in order not to sound an imperialist on a nostalgic journey.

'Have you ridden a camel before?' he asked good-humouredly.

'Only once as a tourist in Wadi Rumm four years ago, and it was the most uncomfortable experience of my life,' I replied.

As he began questioning me about the more practical aspects of the plan, I realised how many details I had overlooked, and how totally dependant on him we were.

'You know,' he said, 'the Bedouin do not do these journeys any more. Our country is changed and only a few remain in the desert. I think perhaps you have come fifty years too late.

'Do you have maps?' he asked.

'No,' I admitted, knowing that James' attempts at astro-navigation would be hopeless without the detailed information they provided.

'We will make a set of maps for you now,' the Brigadier said. It began to look as if the meeting was leading in the right direction. 'I have asked Sheik Hussein, who is the chief of the Howeitat of this area, to meet with us,' he added, reinforcing my optimism. Discreetly the desk bell was pressed and as if on cue a soldier ushered in a well-dressed man in flowing robes. It became obvious that more preparation had gone ahead behind the scenes in Jordan than I had antici-

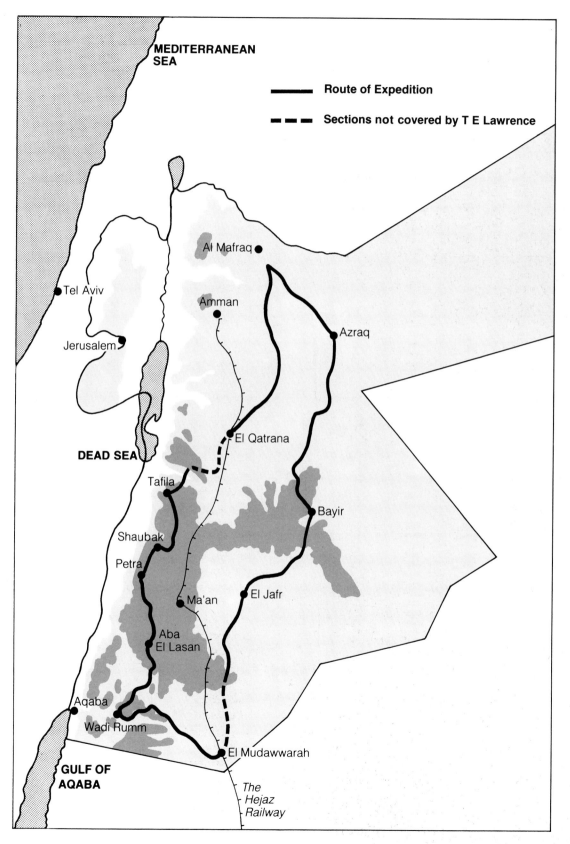

MEDITERRANEAN
SEA

Route of Expedition

Sections not covered by T E Lawrence

Al Mafraq

Tel Aviv

Amman

Azraq

Jerusalem

El Qatrana

DEAD SEA

Tafila

Bayir

Shaubak

Petra

Ma'an

El Jafr

Aba
El Lasan

Aqaba

Wadi Rumm

El Mudawwarah

GULF OF
AQABA

*The
Hejaz
Railway*

pated. We rose to greet the new arrival.

'As-salaam alaykum.' (Peace be upon you.)

'Wa alaykum assalaam.' (And peace be upon you.)

'Kayf haal?' (How are you?)

'Mabsoot, al Hamdu lillaah.' (Well, praise be to God.)

With the formality of the traditional greetings over, a further round of the bitter coffee was drunk. (As is the Arabic custom the pleasantries lasted for some while.) I studied the Sheik, who was younger than I had expected. He wore a pure white kaffiyah (head-dress), and a white robe with a black silk outer garment edged by a broad band of gold lace. His appearance was impeccable. Finally the Brigadier turned to me, and the Sheik accompanied his words with a confident smile of friendship:

'Sheik Hussein here, he has a good man who lives in Wadi Rumm, near Aqaba. His name is Mohammed Musa and he knows plenty about camels. If the price is right he will find the six camels and accompany you on the journey.'

'Shukran,' (Thank you,) I said to the Sheik.

'Ahlan wa sahlan,' (You are welcome,) he replied with a slight bow of his head, then touching his heart, mouth and forehead very briefly in one movement with his right hand. I was moved immediately by the gesture, remembering Tom Beaumont's words that this meant he was saying 'In my heart I feel no evil towards you; my mouth will speak no evil of you; and in my mind I will think nothing but good things about you.'

We talked for a while of the price for the camels and the food needed for them and ourselves. It was finally agreed to hire the six camels rather than buy them outright. We would hire them from Mohammed Musa and he would be responsible for their care. At such a late stage it was the only solution since the price of one animal alone was nearly £2,000 and there was hardly one hour to spare before setting out into the desert. To decline the proffered assistance and haggle instead among other Howeitat

tribesmen might have taken up to a fortnight to achieve a satisfactory result. The large sum of £1,000 would be paid for each camel for five weeks including the necessary grain required for their feeding. Mohammed Musa would be paid £400.

At this juncture the bell was rung again and the man called Mohammed Musa entered. His clothes told the story of the life of the true desert tribesman. I felt alien in my clean trousers, shirt and tie. His face was rugged, his eyes were powerful and brilliant: Mohammed had the countenance of a shrewd hawk. As I sat at the opposite end of the office I understood Lawrence's delight in describing such meetings. As a military man I had the feeling of being a brand new officer meeting his seasoned platoon sergeant for the first time. The Brigadier and Sheik Hussein explained the earlier negotiations to Mohammed. He looked from one to the other, missing nothing and occasionally looking at me as though I were responsible for the complications. He did not smile until the agreement had been completed.

At the moment of decision he looked at me and formed his opinion; I returned the look and formed my own. His eyes knew me, but I did not, as yet, know him.

We left, having arranged to meet Mohammed in Aqaba the following morning. The Brigadier had offered us the government rest house, an old Colonial bungalow on the beach, for the duration of our stay and we would move into it directly. The provisions and Arab clothing were to be purchased under Mohammed's guidance and the expedition would join him in Wadi Rumm as soon as possible. In my imagination I began at last to see the Arabian desert nights.

'Mohammed looks quite a character,' Colonel David remarked as we drove through the hills back to the bustling sea port.

'Yes, I was thinking that... It is going to be quite an education.' For the first time I was not sure whether I was going to enjoy it.

Chapter One

14 February

Mohammed Musa squats in the sand beside the small hearth fire. Between his feet is wedged a brass mortar, as rhythmically he pounds the roasted coffee beans with a pestle. I am woken by the resonant bell-like sound as he strikes the sides of the heavy bowl. Over the fire is a shallow open pan on which some beans are being roasted. With the aroma of coffee and the ringing echoes of Mohammed's pounding, I lie quiet and relaxed in the darkness of the black tent. From the warmth and comfort of my sleeping bag I casually note the emerging details of a desert dawn with a Bedouin family. It is the first day of the expedition.

I study Mohammed first, the image of his face distorted by the flickering shadows from the firelight. His head-dress or 'kaffiyah', a cloth patterned with small red and white squares which is swept back to the sides in a cascade of material, effectively conceals the outline of his head and shoulders. Two coils of thick black cord hold it firmly in place as he bends forward in his work. His face is gaunt and lined, with deep furrows on his forehead and sagging skin about his eyes. The grey tinge of chin stubble, and the wisps of grey hair protruding from beneath his kaffiyah, confirm his advancing years. His eyes reflect the firelight, and I sense the wisdom which years of harshness and suffering have accumulated. Covering the rest of him is a brown robe edged with a thick band of gold lining, and I wonder if it has any significance to his status in the Howeitat tribe to which he belongs. He looks noble, yet there is a gentle humility in his actions. It is as though he has an inbred resignation to the daily toil of life and an acceptance of the slow, menial but important domestic tasks.

As he methodically prepares the coffee, I realise Mohammed knows few of the conveniences of the Western world. He is a desert nomad, his way of life scarcely remains in the modern world and its preservation inspires a wonderful sense of stability and integrity. As I watch him it seems to me as though he has pushed everything I know far away. Occasionally he stops pounding and puts the bowl to one side. Still squatting, he moves closer to the fire for warmth and holds his gnarled hands over its small flame.

'Sabaah al-khair,' I venture none too confident of my pronunciation.

Mohammed squints through the fire smoke and fixes me with his small sharp eyes. He nods grunts and replies 'Sabaah an-noor.'

The conversation goes no further than these morning greetings. I speak insufficient Arabic to handle little more than polite
but rather simple questions, and somehow to ask him if he slept
well sounds out of place. I want to convey my happiness at being
a guest in his tent in the desert, and how pleased I am that the
camels will be loaded this morning for our planned departure. I
want to ask him of the arrangements for this and the six camels
and other Bedouin who will accompany us. We have seen
nothing of either since our arrival in Wadi Rumm the previous
evening.

I try again, 'Kayf haalak Mohammed?'

He replies that he is well indeed, thanks be to God. This time
he beckons me to the fire to drink tea with him*. The blackened
kettle balancing on an iron trestle has already boiled. Mohammed opens a dirty cloth bag in the sand at his feet and carefully
scoops out two handfuls of tea, which he adds one at a time to the
kettle. Last night I discovered how very sweet the Bedouin drink
their tea, and usually the cupfulls of sugar are added before the
water boils. It was refreshing, up to the third glass, but they
appear to drink it with a frequency and dedication worthy of
addicts.

I squat by the fire opposite Mohammed and try to imitate his
position. Before very long my Western upbringing prevents me
from feeling like a native, and the discomfort in my joints forces
me to sit on the sand, legs crossed, attempting to maintain a
suitable dignity and poise. Mohammed continues to pound the
coffee beans seemingly oblivious of my presence, while I sip the
tea from a small glass (Duralex, made in France, I note).

The dawn outside is pale and cold.

I should feel inspired and uplifted by our situation and surroundings - warrior Bedouins, *Beau Geste* scenery, the desert
dawn, and Englishmen following the romantic legend of
Lawrence of Arabia. I try, yet somehow it feels natural to be with
Mohammed's family in the desert, and Heathrow Airport, where
we had been less than four days ago, seems to belong to a different
age. Furthermore the black tents of the Bedouin in Wadi Rumm
are not miles from anywhere. A badly pot-holed road connects it
to the main Amman to Aqaba highway, and the beauty of Rumm
is high on the agenda of many tourists in Jordan. This ease of
access to the Bedouin world has removed the expectation I had of
it being an immediate sanctuary. True there exists with the
Bedouin a traditional life-style barely changed over the centuries,
but what of the Toyota pick-ups parked beside the camels and
goats behind the tents? Should I turn a blind eye to them in order
to maintain the impressions I formed in my mind during the
planning of the expedition, impressions of a desert unchanged by
encroaching technology? The fact that Japanese vehicles are an
accepted part of desert life saddens me, but as I watch Moham-

---

*Coffee is always served before the sweet tea and therefore an invitation to drink one will naturally
involve staying for both.

med in his morning routine I realise that they have not fundamentally altered his life as a desert nomad. His existence is timeless.

The coffee is ready. Using his hands as a funnel, Mohammed pours the fine brown powder into an antique-looking brass jug with a tapering neck and a long curved spout. When the boiling water is added the aroma of coffee in the tent is even stronger. Very deliberately he positions the jug by the edge of the fire in the grey cinders. There is no conversation. Mohammed I suspect has an English vocabulary of roughly twenty words, and since my Arabic is limited to the same amount, I continue to take in my surroundings.

The tent is made from goat hair. It is black and coarse, woven into long strips which are then sewn together by rope. Two parallel white bands run along its length near to the ground. I remember reading once that white symbolizes that a particular family had repaid a past debt, and that the stain on their honour had been washed away. The tent is rectangular in shape with a partition dividing it in two, and it is from behind the screen that I can hear Mohammed's wife in the cooking area. She coughs continually, and I hope the clatter of pans indicates some food is being prepared. Except for the three inert forms of the expedition members in their sleeping bags on the ground, the remainder of the tent is relatively bare. Beside them is a deep pile of rugs which is the bed of Mohammed's fifteen-year-old son, Salem. It is 5 am. No one else has stirred.

My eyes water from the wood smoke. After only one night the smell of smoke has permeated my hair and clothes. I feel dirty and a foul taste lingers in my mouth. We have come to live as Bedouins, and I wonder what condition we will be in after a month in the desert with limited water and food, and wearing the same clothes.

Lifting the curtain, which had been hung last night to protect the open side, I go out to watch the sunrise. The only sound is the stirring solo of an occasional cockerel, and the coughing and gurgling from a nearby camel. Here and there blue smoke seeps through the other Howeitat tents in the small settlement of Rumm. The day begins early - the routine of the other families no different to that of Mohammed and his wife. There is no movement outside the tents, of which there are about a dozen interspersed between a few concrete and tin huts of recent and poor design.

The sand is fine and cold to my bare feet. I look about for a suitable place to relieve myself. There is none. For the first time I wonder what the Bedouin do, especially living here for much of the year. The nearest rocks are a few hundred yards away, and except for the odd small undulation of sand and camel thorn bush, there is no cover. The tents of the other families are in easy view of any single area of the wadi's bottom, and my immediate fear is whether I would be offending Bedouin custom by relieving myself in the near vicinity. I gaze at the magnificence of the high rock buttresses flanking the wadi. Certainly the greatest fear is being caught exposed by a woman: women traditionally will not even be seen in the family tent by male guests. Boldly I decide to head for the nearest bush and turn my back on the tents.

The stone fort of the desert police post is the largest and most permanent man-made feature in the wadi. It is surrounded by a few evergreen trees, and with its whitewashed parapets and wooden sentry box it looks as though it is part of a Hollywood film set. I study it with interest as I walk back to the tent, realising that the last time I had seen it in daylight was in 1981 while briefly attached to the Jordanian Army. Also it reminds me of the enigmatic events which occurred in the evening soon after our arrival at Mohammed's tent:

Shortly after we had finished a large 'mensaf'- the traditional Arabic feast of sheep's meat served on a sizeable dish and heaped with local bread or rice - a member of the desert police had come to Mohammed's tent summoning him to the fort. One hour later he still had not returned. We were unsure of our status in Wadi Rumm, but felt that Mohammed's absence must somehow be related to the arrangements for our departure in the morning. Therefore, in a darkness punctuated with vivid stars, James and I walked towards the shadowed, small stone fort to find out what was happening. We drew on the confidence of our upbringing and assumed the air of travellers accustomed to petty problems and officials.

The sentry escorted us inside the fort where the blaze of the fire revealed an open tent with a row of men in uniform seated on Persian rugs and cushions. Either squatting or sitting cross-legged in the sand opposite them, and ranged in a semi-circle about the fire, were nearly a dozen Bedu and some off-duty members of the police post. Our sudden appearance out of the darkness silenced the gathering. Their heads turned and they rose to greet us solemnly. Mohammed stood with the remainder and watched us keenly as we approached the group. Light from the fire flickered, caressing them in a kaleidoscope of colour, exaggerating their flowing robes and highlighting the polished rows of bullets worn by the policemen in crossed leather straps over their khaki uniforms.

It was immediately apparent from the strained atmosphere that we were interrupting something which was not our business. We moved around the circle shaking hands with each man, muttering greetings and admitting that God was indeed responsible for our good health.

'Chief he no want me go,' Mohammed said quietly when I reached him. Before I could ask why, the sergeant - the 'Chief' Mohammed referred to - motioned us to sit beside him. There was an obvious interest in our presence as we sat and faced the colourful, roguish audience. They stopped talking among themselves and strained forwards to listen as the sergeant began questioning me closely on the price paid for the services of Mohammed and for each camel. My honest answers, half in Arabic and half in English, were then given over for general discussion. The Bedu had the look of a self-appointed jury. Before very long they were shouting loudly. Mohammed argued his case aggressively, counter-attacked, smiling and laughing provocatively. He remained the centre of the proceedings. Soon it was obvious that we were involved in a fine point of tribal politics.

As we sat it became apparent that the Bedu were in some way connected with the camels and the price arranged for their hire. Whatever Mohammed had done was the bone of contention. As the senior man in rank the police sergeant was seeking opinions on the issue before casting his verdict. Irrespective of status or familiarity with the facts of the case, nearly everyone was having his own say. They all spoke together. None listened. Such was their fervour that one would have thought each man's personal livelihood depended on the outcome. As aliens to the language and uncertain of the tone of the discussion, we waited, silent onlookers, propped on our elbows among the embroidered cushions. Mohammed and the sergeant faced each other over the fire. They both played with strings of worry beads and drew on their cigarettes hungrily as the intensity of the argument increased.

Mohammed's brother was our only insight into the evening's events. His bulky frame and pale face disclosed the easy life of the town Arab. In fair English he translated the discussion which left us more confused than before.

We were scrutinized by inquisitive eyes but never asked for our opinions; I felt as the perpetrator of a hideous crime must feel when unable to defend himself. So it continued for over an hour. We quietly feared that the outcome of the issue, which was being decided by these unknown people, would affect the success of our expedition. The tea cups were constantly refilled and we smoked frequent cigarettes to reduce our feeling of unease and conceal our nakedness in such a foreign affair.

Eventually Mohammed simply stood up, nodded to the sergeant and walked off with a backward beckoning glance. We politely excused ourselves, shook hands once more with each man and thankfully allowed the darkness to cover our withdrawal from a situation that was obviously beyond our control. Later, grouped together like conspirators outside the fort, Mohammed's brother explained that the police chief wanted an equal distribution of money to all parties who had placed their camels in Mohammed's hands. Mohammed was arguing that this was contrary to the agreement reached with Sheik Hussein and Brigadier Shobaky the previous day. Furthermore, the sergeant warned that until he was satisfied, the expedition was not to leave the wadi. James and I were unable to decide whether Mohammed had innocently misinterpreted the agreement or was in fact on a deliberate fiddle for the largest share. But we certainly admired his single-handed defence against such formidable opponents.

With these thoughts in mind I return to the tent. The confusion and uncertainty of last night's wranglings reminds me that a settlement will have to be reached soon, particularly since the expedition is booked to return to England in little over a month. On entering the tent, I decide to speak to Mohammed once the sun is risen. Inside it is surprisingly warm after the dawn chill.

Mohammed ignores my return. He appears more reserved about us in comparison to yesterday's generous reception. As I watch him stir Salem to fetch more water and wood, I wonder if he regards our presence and the entire situation as a nuisance to his family and their way of life. Sleepily Salem leaves the tent. Mohammed then casually removes his white cotton trousers from under his robes, and without looking throws them over his shoulder to land squarely on the dividing partition. Their progress is accompanied by a curt order to his unseen wife. A hand quickly retrieves them. Almost immediately a clean pair sail back over and catch Mohammed on the head. I smile at the sight. Mohammed merely takes them without a word of thanks, and I cannot help thinking that the Bedu have their wives well trained.

'More tea?' he enquires once he is dressed again. I find the third cup is enjoyable along with the second cigarette of the day. It is now 5.30 am. The sun has just begun to touch the very tips of the highest peaks of Wadi Rumm, revealing pinnacles of rock changing from a pale red to yellow. The shadow of dawn seems to shrink down the rock with every second. I watch through a gap in the tent as the sky changes from dull grey to a gentle blue and the slow unveiling of the sandstone hills amazes me. Mohammed notices nothing.

Behind me in the shadows of the tent a match is struck. I turn to see the flame illuminate James' unkempt face, remembering from our previous expedition how he would always light a cigarette before leaving his sleeping bag. I envy the amount of sleep he has enjoyed since I had not returned to the tent until 2 am. Having left James behind, I had driven with Mohammed and his brother to speak with Sheik Hussein in Guweira. The small village was 30 miles away but Mohammed confidently predicted that the sheik would solve the camel problem. I sat wedged between the two Arabs in the front of a battered landrover as we raced across the desert in the dead of night. They talked constantly in an excited jabber.

I merely sat in the middle like a small innocent boy glancing from one to the other, not understanding a thing. At one stage a desert fox was dazzled by the headlights, and we drove off the road in a chase across the sand that nearly ended with the landrover on its side.

Somehow I had expected a sheik to be living in a splendid tent.

Above: *The press conference in the camel enclosure at Whipsnade Zoo, England.*

Right: *'The afternoon air was hot and still in the Wadi Araba on 11 February, 1985. The white embassy landrover with CD plates, was parked on the sandy verge where it had halted, out of fuel, "as God had willed"...40 miles later it coughed to a second halt just beside a Jordanian army border position dug into the hillside. Those of us able to raise a smile on the first day of acclimatisation, stranded somewhere between the Dead Sea and Aqaba, shared the feeling that at least the camels would not have such mechanical shortcomings.'*

Left: *Preparing to embark on the expedition at Wadi Rumm. 'By now several people have gathered by the tents where preparations for our departure are at last gathering pace. This colourful and exciting scene is made complete by the arrival of the last two camels, the silent pads of their feet raising small dust clouds in the sand, their walk gentle and controlled, a steady rhythm of strength... We are now the centre of attention in the wadi, and with Arabs this means that each of us in turn receives a fair measure of eagerly imparted advice.'*

Above: *'It is our first close contact with camels since being chased across the snow by some of their hideous relatives at Whipsnade Zoo. We turn to look, fascinated by these "ships of the desert"... James is dressed in baggy khaki trousers and army sweater, and on his feet are heavy military boots. He makes me feel hot just to look at him. I take a photograph as he approaches Mohammed's camel. The expression on both faces as they meet for the first time is an enquiring and respectful one...'*

Stage 1: *departing Wadi Rumm for El Mudawwarah. On riding into Wadi Rumm, Lawrence wrote, 'Day was still young as we rode between two great pikes of sandstone to the foot of a long, soft slope poured down from the domed hills in front of us. It was tamarisk-covered: the beginning of the Valley of Rumm, they said. We looked up on the left to a long wall of rock, sheering in like a thousand-foot wave towards the middle of the valley... The Arab armies would have been lost in the length and breadth of it, and within the walls a squadron of aeroplanes could have wheeled in formation.'*

Instead we found Hussein's home to be one of the better buildings among the shabby collection in Guweira. Inside it was
sparse, yet outside on the unsurfaced road stood his immaculate
white Mercedes. The sheik was apologetic for the problem of
paying for the camels and immediately rang Brigadier Shobaky
to solve it. The Brigadier was out. We waited two hours and tried
again, but this time the sheik's telephone was broken. Undeter-
red we drove 10 miles to the King's Highway to the nearest
telephone - it was the emergency one by the road. Sheik Hussein
had only to mention his name and Shobaky's and he had a free
call.

Sitting in the Mercedes with the four others, the sheik talking
from the comfort of his seat and the juggernauts hurtling to and
fro to Aqaba, I felt far away from the desert and the legend of
Lawrence. I felt guilty about disturbing the Commander of the
Southern Military Area at midnight, and at the same time
impressed by the personal interest and care he took for the well-
being of four British soldiers. It was established that he was
powerless to solve our dilemma until the morning, but, more
important, Mohammed was happier knowing he had found an
ally in the Brigadier. As we waited upon his deliberations, I made
the fatal error of admiring Mohammed's ivory worry beads. He
promptly gave them to me as a present. It took much strenuous
persuasion to convince him that I was merely admiring their age
and colour and that in my society it did not mean I wanted them.
I am recounting this to James as the others wake up and join us
by the fire. They are both quiet and look tentatively at their
surroundings and companions.

Breakfast is a simple affair, sweet tea with large strips of thin
bread not unlike chamois leather. Both Chris and Mark look
nonplussed. They are the youngest and least travelled of the
expedition members. We have known each other only three days.
There remains an awkwardness on their part to be on such close
terms with two officers of their own regiment. I want them to mix
in and be at ease, to ask questions and absorb this way of life.
Their faces remain guarded and they smile politely. It was a
point Lawrence had noted in *Seven Pillars of Wisdom* that Englishmen among the Arabs tended to become more insular and
English when confronted with these alien and strange ways.

Mohammed picks some bread off the sacking cover in the sand.
This approximation of a tablecloth amuses me. He allows the
bread to hang from his fingers and warms first one side and then
the other, at flame height. The bread is light brown with dark
speckles and seemingly transparent in places. It is chewy and
tasteless. With a glass of tea, it is all that is on offer. James and I
remark that it is as well we smoke to fill the gap. Mark suggests a
diet will improve his figure, and Chris that as a follower of some
Japanese martial art he is used to sparse living.

There are now four camels outside Mohammed's tent. Each has

its front legs roped or 'hobbled' together to prevent it from wandering. Two are tied to the rough piles of bleached firewood that define a close perimeter about the tent; the other two lie couched in the sand. They are all bulls and appear smaller than the ones we had seen in England.

It is our first close contact with camels since being chased across the snow by some of their hideous relatives at Whipsnade Zoo. We turn to look, fascinated by these 'ships of the desert' that will be carrying us one thousand miles around Jordan. Suddenly one of the camels leans his head back, and simultaneously a large pink tongue, alive and slobbering, spills from the left side of his mouth, almost a foot long. The camel's head shakes. The pinkness fills with air causing different areas to inflate and deflate in ripples - each expansion is accompanied by a deep gurgling that sounds like the repulsive intermittent snoring of a dirty old man. It hangs, spent, and then almost immediately comes alive again to repeat the performance. The sight looks ridiculous to us. However the camel maintains a serene expression, his large unblinking eyes regarding us with indifference perhaps even disdain. James thinks the camel is mad and I give it to him to ride as he has had more experience of camels than the rest of us.

He chuckles, the inevitable cigarette held by those long thin fingers is placed between his lips and his eyes are smiling. James often has this mischievous look. He is dressed in baggy khaki trousers and army sweater, and on his feet are heavy military boots. He makes me feel hot just to look at him. I take a photograph as he approaches Mohammed's camel. The expression on both faces as they meet head-on is an enquiring and respectful one, mingled with a touch of humorous anticipation on James' side.

By now several people have gathered by the tents where the preparations for our departure are at last gathering pace. This colourful and exciting scene is completed by the arrival of the last two camels (one a small female or nagar) and their owners, the silent pads of the camels' feet raising small dust clouds in the sand, their walk gentle and controlled, a steady rhythm of strength. It has its moment.

However, we are in glaring contrast to this native, desert scene. Our gaudy western commodities embarrass me - the blue and white bags with 'Rothmans' emblazoned across their length, the lurid orange tripod that will mount our theodolite for astro-navigation, large green sleeping bags, hooped bivvy bags (a form of one-man tent) and green and blue windproof smocks. I scrutinise the clumsy pile outside the tent, realising that at this point, East and West meet. These people survive on nothing and have precious few material possessions. They are in harmony with their environment. We are intruders, vulnerable in our naivety and overburdened with resources.

I look at the equipment strewn outside Mohammed's tent and realise how ridiculous it is. Despite the fact that a camel can carry its own weight, I know we must reduce our bulk if we are to travel quickly. The expedition aim is to dress and live exactly as Arabs - a Rothmans bag hanging off my saddle will do nothing to enhance that image.

I gather the team around and we begin to redistribute our personal effects and the essential expedition kit. Everyone sighs resignedly, for only yesterday morning in Aqaba I had gone through the same ritual, inspecting all equipment and disregarding anything deemed unnecessary. My instructions are one bag between two and the surplus to be left with Mohammed's family. I want to be positive and eliminate all comforts. I am impatient to shed our Western identity and became one of the Bedouin as soon as possible. They have no such things as bivvy bags therefore these will be left behind. Each man will carry his own survival rations and medical pack, one pair of socks, five pairs of paper pants, a thick sweater, and one set of clothing only - initially the Arab robes will be worn over our desert khaki. Knowing there will be insufficient water I tell them to leave their washing and shaving kit too. There are now two piles of equipment, the essentials and the non-essentials. It is beginning to look more like an expedition and less like a package holiday.

Meanwhile assisted by his wife and son, Mohammed is busy preparing the camels for loading. Already centralised are four sacks of grain, a sack of flour, smaller sacks of tea, salt and sugar, cooking pots and a kettle, some blankets and some apparently moth-eaten sheepskin rugs, bags of hard bread rolls and two small plastic water containers. From large strips of rough cloth they make sacks to accommodate our equipment thus camouflaging the hallmarks of more conventional travellers.

A Jordanian army major comes across to introduce himself. Brigadier Shobaky has sent him to ensure our safe and smooth departure, he informs me. Eight Schermuley distress flares and an emergency Dayglo panel to attract aircraft are handed over too. We each carry letters of safe conduct guaranteeing our free movement through the military areas, and explaining the nature of the journey. These, he emphasises, must be shown at every desert police post which will be our only method of remaining in contact.

We are now the centre of attention in the wadi, and with Arabs this means that each of us in turn receives a fair measure of eagerly imparted advice. It seems the loading of the camels is being done by everyone. The sacks come on and off the saddles and are redistributed according to the individual characteristics of the camels. These characteristics it seems are known to everyone. It is becoming hot and dusty and as with the previous evening's discussions, we have no role to play.

Each riding saddle is wooden. It sits centrally over the hump of the camel and is held firm by a girth woven from goat hair. The saddle has two tapered bone pommels front and rear, and the centre of the seat itself is open in order not to actually squash the hump flat. It is from these pommels that the brown sacks of equipment and provisions hang suspended by rope. The camels are loaded while couched. They register the addition of each bulky sack with a disapproving display of yellowing teeth and pitiful moans. Each camel carries approximately two sacks on either side, and then a saddle bag of woven cloth disguises the overall effect with its bright colours and hanging tassels. The final touch is the padding of the saddle with sheepskin rugs.

'Where go?' the staff officer asks. I produce a large map of Jordan from the side of my saddle bag. Everyone crowds round as I trace with my finger the route of our first leg to El Mudawwarah 50 miles to the south-east.

'Mundawarrah...ha,' someone repeats correcting my pronunciation. I repeat it. Someone else corrects me. The small crowd gathers closer. Soon each man is gesticulating, fingers pointing and advising on the route with the same tenacious belief in their individual knowledge that they had shown over the loading of the camels.

I trace in the remainder of the route that encompasses much of the Jordanian desert - from El Jafr to Bayir, Azraq, east to the Arabian border and south to the Wadi ash Sirhan, north again to Azraq, Mafrak and returning south via Shaubak and Petra to either Wadi Rumm or Aqaba. My pronunciation is wrong again. Obediently I repeat my corrections to the smiling advisers who identify themselves by touching my arm or shoulder. The staff officer writes the route down and asks in Arabic how many days it will be to El Mudawwarah. This being within my limited repertoire I reply in the same tongue that it will take two days - God willing. Those that are close enough to hear, smile at my acceptance of Arab fatalism.

'Awah,' they chorus, 'in shaa Allah, in shaa Allah!' A wizened old man comes forward. His face is twisted, the long hawkish nose emphasised by his dirty white kaffiyah. He takes my hand.

'Hashan...Hashan.' I look, uncomprehending. He leans closer and involuntarily I recoil at the smell of bad breath from his rotten teeth.

'Hashan, me,' he repeats, this time pointing a crooked finger at his chest and then towards the singularly bored looking camel by my side. I understand now. Yet one hour earlier another man had been equally proud to claim ownership of Hashan. Perhaps they own one end each, I conclude silently.

'Good, Hashan is good. Thank you,' I reply. He smiles and nods a few times. The assembled onlookers also smile as if to share his pride or perhaps to celebrate my breakthrough in communication.

Suddenly there is a great deal of movement that raises a dust cloud. One by one the camels rise to their feet with their uncertain looking riders pitching forwards and backwards with the motion. It is the first time for Chris and Mark and they look surprised to be so far above the ground, but equally relieved that

Chris on his camel for the first time.

'One by one the camels rise to their feet with their uncertain looking riders pitching forwards and backwards with the motion.'

Mark accustoming himself to his camel.

'The heat of Arabia came out like a drawn sword, and struck us speechless.'
Seven Pillars of Wisdom

they have not yet been thrown off or bitten. Mark had remarked bravely at the press conference that he had not even ridden a donkey, let alone a camel.

Mohammed walks across and I notice he is dressed no differently from this morning. I begin to realise that this journey is probably no more to him than moving his family and sheep from one part of the desert to another in search of grazing. He informs me that we are ready to leave and that Abdulla, a young sulky boy I had met the previous night, and Hamad Awad will also accompany us until we are competent with the camels. He assures me that they will leave after that.

I prepare to mount Hashan with Mohammed's assistance. The staff officer shakes hands and wishes us good luck. I bid farewell to the police sergeant whose smile tells me that last night's problem has been sorted out to everyone's satisfaction. But he does not look totally at ease.

With a deep groan and a jarring lurch forward, Hashan raises his rear legs. I hang on tightly to the front pommel only to jolt sharply backwards as the weight is finally taken on the front legs. It really does seem a long way off the ground.

The caravan picks its way through the tents and animal pens of the settlement at Rumm. We are heading into the sun towards the opening of the wadi where the sandstone buttresses finally appear to relax their hold on the desert. The three Bedu lead the camels by the head rope. They occasionally wave goodbye to friends but the overall impression is that they are taking tourists for the normal jaunt up the wadi to a site named 'Lawrence's Spring'.

Without any of us having said or done anything, it seems that the expedition has safely begun. It occurs to me, though, that there are precious few water containers being·carried by the camels. Without knowing what to expect in the next thousand miles, I am convinced that if we carry adequate water then at least there is a chance of survival should the worst occur. Feeling very much like a small boy asking a publican if he sells beer, I ask Mohammed if he has sufficient as I only saw two small containers. He stops walking and comes around the side of the camel.

'You want more water?' he asks as he looks up and shields his eyes from the glaring sun.

'Yes,' I reply simply. Surprisingly he immediately turns to his son, who alone of the advisers of five minutes ago is accompanying us to the last tent, and issues rapid instructions. Five minutes later Salem returns with two large blue plastic jerrycans. With their white screw-on caps they are not quite the image of the goat-skin water carriers I had expected. Mohammed halts at a well on the outskirts of the village. Once filled, the containers are hung from the front and rear pommels of one of the riderless camels. They do look incongruous. Nevertheless I feel more relaxed about our water supply, if just a little disconcerted that we should have been leaving with only two small containers between seven and which were empty in the first place.

I smile at Mark who sits astride his camel in the manner of a rodeo rider. James has the largest camel and the animal's split nostril seems to emit a loud whistling noise each time a breath is exhaled. The combination of this and his large rubbery jaws, the lower lip flapping up and down with the motion of his stride, make me think that we will have one camel who will provide a certain amount of entertainment. This is confirmed when he throws back his head, and to the accompaniment of a loud gurgling sound his slobbering pink tongue drops from the side of his mouth. It is the second time this morning, and we laugh at the comical sight. The three Bedu laugh at our curiosity at this seemingly eccentric behaviour, and then Mohammed points to some smaller female camels grazing nearby. He makes an obscene gesture and laughs without any inhibition; it seems that James' camel not only looks mad but also has a strong sexual drive.

We move out into the unblemished desert where the sand is a fine red colour with a sparse covering of small thorn bushes - unblemished, provided one ignores the plastic bags and litter blown from Rumm that fix themselves on the bushes as if to clothe them. Ahead a small dust cloud swirls from one side of the wadi to the other as we begin to follow a well incised track of tyre marks in the sand.

I feel a tremendous surge of excitement as I survey the scene; mingled with it is a sense of disbelief that the year of planning and false hopes are behind me and the expedition has actually begun. Elation at finding the camels, the Bedouin and free access through all military areas in only four days, more than compensates for the disappointment in not going to Saudi. I settle more comfortably into Hashan's saddle.

Suddenly Mohammed halts, turns to face the distant tents and shouts loudly. The small figure of Salem hurriedly runs towards us, arriving breathless and a little wide eyed. Mohammed says little and merely takes out a cloth bundle from under his robe and counts a number of well worn bank notes. He gives these to Salem,and after a few more words pulls on Hashan's head rope and begins his journey. Salem turns to walk back to the tents. Neither look back.

Chapter Two

'Our little caravan grew self-conscious, and fell dead quiet, afraid and ashamed to flaunt its smallness in the presence of the stupendous hills,' wrote Lawrence in *Seven Pillars of Wisdom* about the walls of Rumm. It is a feeling the soldiers of the eighties share as we ride in silence through awe-inspiring scenery. We meander between the sandstone outcrops in a generally south-easterly direction. The colour of the sand is ever-changing from fine red to pale yellow and in areas a greyish white. The horizontal strata of the rock encourages us forward. Mostly it is a smoothed sculpture but there are sharp cracks and rifts where the rock has moved and only dark and shifting shadows live.

We are silent, dwarfed by nature and, I feel, timeless amongst it all. Mohammed leads his own camel on foot while behind him Abdulla leads James and Chris with the spare camel tied to James' saddle. Mark and I, on the last two camels, are with Hamad whom I do not trust at the moment. He looks a simple man, yet he has shifty eyes. His walk is more of a shamble. Occasionally he looks around and smiles asking if everything is good. My reply is positive and he smiles again as if he knows something I do not.

The Guweira plain, leaving Wadi Rumm.

'Our little caravan grew self-conscious, and fell dead quiet, afraid and ashamed to flaunt its smallness in the presence of the stupendous hills.' Seven Pillars of Wisdom

En route to El Mudawwarah, leaving the hills of Rumm.

'The mark of nomadism, that most deep and biting social discipline, was on each of them to his degree.' Seven Pillars of Wisdom

The route is the same one Lawrence took in September 1917. He led a raiding party of two hundred Arabs, leaving from Rumm to blow up the strategic Hejaz railway south of El Mudawwarah. In this he was successful. Today, the same Turkish troop train lies on its side in the sand by the disused line and it is our intention to reach it. I feel a thrill of anticipation at the thought of standing beside such a relic, particularly since the expedition is the first of its kind to retrace Lawrence's journeys in the manner in which he lived and fought the Arab revolt.

Mohammed leads on. He assures me that he knows the route to El Mudawwarah and that it is the one Lawrence followed. With our limited command of Arabic we cannot find out how he knows this, but I presume it is an ancient camel trading route. In this way we are likely to be following Lawrence exactly.

Mark cries in alarm. His camel has slumped down while in full walking stride. Hamad coaxes the reluctant animal up. Mark settles once more and tries to take a photograph - an impossible task as I had discovered in the past hour. Giving that up he begins to hum loudly the theme tune of the film *Lawrence of Arabia*. We smile. For the first time the scene does conjure up romantic notions and legends.

There is another cry from behind and Mark is down again. His camel is snarling and moaning and the volume of complaint increases with the sharp strokes from Hamad's stick. This time Mark hangs on to the front pommel with both hands. Now he looks most disconcerted and is complaining that every time he relaxes, the camel simply sinks to the sand. We are at the

James has the largest camel.

'Bicycles they called devil-horses, the children of cars, which themselves were sons and daughters of trains...' Seven Pillars of Wisdom

beginning of a slow learning process, and from Mark's experience with his mount, a month in their company will be a long time.

After four hours we halt near a rock overhang with an ample covering of tamarisk in front. We are sore from riding, and a blister has begun to form on my backside from the constant friction of the saddle. Dismounting with relief, we assist the Bedu in unloading the sacks. It is hot. The tubes of sunscreen and 'Factor 6' do the rounds with the exception of James, who scorns such 'effeminacy'. Every time we move to assist the Bedu with a camel or loads we are chided. With our status as complete amateurs confirmed, we happily allow them to continue and rest for a few minutes to study our surroundings in detail.

Abdulla begins to move a couple of grain sacks under the rock ledge, following them with blankets and his magnificent sheepskin jacket. The enthusiasm with which he surveys it as a bed is suspicious. He says something unintelligible to Hamad who appears to agree, and Mohammed is quietly lighting a fire to boil the water. I decide to watch and wait but nevertheless mutter my misgivings to James. It would seem that Abdulla and Hamad are ready to remain here for the night but there are at least two hours of daylight left for travelling, and at the most we can have only covered 12 miles. The expedition's aim is 1,000 miles. That means a minimum of 30 miles a day. I begin to feel trapped.

'Captain, Captain...Sleep here, sleep here,' Abdulla says in broken English. It confirms our worst fears. My pulse quickens with the prospect of a confrontation in an alien country with three strange Bedu, on whose goodwill the success of the journey is entirely dependant. Ignoring him I busily scour the sand for more tamarisk twigs.

'Captain, sleep here...yes?' he shouts again. The first test has come. I walk to the fire and face the three Arabs.

'No. No sleep here,' I reply in a firm voice. 'Mohammed, two more hours then sleep.' The order is deliberately aimed at Mohammed, implying that he is the chief camel handler, and I hope to hear what he feels. Abdulla now looks very sulky. Mohammed continues to make the tea from which he does not even look up.

'Mister, camel is tired, camel is hungry,' whines Abdulla again. I ignore him, silently appalled at this attitude from the legendary Howeitat.

James suggests wearing our Bedouin clothing now that we have left Rumm. We delve into the sacks and self-consciously put on the long thobe which is like an unflattering ankle-length dress, then meticulously inspect the jaunty angles of each others' kaffiyahs. We shyly join the Bedu by the fire, but feel a little more acceptable nonetheless. They do not appear to think we are trying to be something we are not and welcome our new clothes, and smiling, hand around glasses of tea. The camels graze behind us with their front legs hobbled and the head ropes tethering them to the tamarisk. The act is complete, but the tension and uncertainty remain.

'Mohammed, no stay here,' I repeat looking him straight in the eyes as we squat on opposing sides of the now grey ash of the fire. He tut-tuts loudly. Beside him Abdulla slurps his tea noisily adding to my sense of frustration.

'How far you go?' Mohammed inquires and silently points to some darkening clouds to the north. I consult my watch.

'One hour, maybe 5 kilometres.' At least that would be something.

'Mister...look Mister,' Abdulla whines again, 'camel is tired, we tired...walking, walking.' Of the three he speaks the most English. 'Captain, you must slowly, slowly for camel.'

Trying to keep the sternness from my voice I ask how far we can cover in one day. Abdulla replies in Arabic that it is 20 kilometres, perhaps, God willing. Frustration and anger rise together as I sense how they are trying to manipulate us in order to make their lives easy. I decide to postpone an argument about distance until later. The aim is to win the first battle of will, and to travel for even one hour would prove the point. In shaa Allah. Finally I say we will go on further and stand up, telling the others to begin packing the sacks. Meanwhile the Bedu continue to drink their tea. I fear the expedition is splitting into two parties on only the first day, but then to my relief, Mohammed says something and Abdulla retrieves the grain sacks and his belongings.

Rightly or wrongly a little mastery of the situation has been established - at what cost, I wonder, as I lead off. The caravan follows the course of a flat-bottomed valley between the darkening lines of hills. The light is fading. We walk and lead our own camels to show a measure of our resolve and consideration for the animals too. After one day without any proper food I begin to feel very hungry as I walk at the front, determined to stretch the pace and achieve a maximum distance. Looking behind I notice that Hamad and Abdulla are riding. I curse.

It begins to rain lightly, and I feel ridiculed and wonder whether Mohammed is not looking at my back thinking 'I told you so for all your Western arrogance and impatience.'

'Charles! Charles!' I stop and look back. James is indicating that Mohammed has turned off and is heading for the rocks. We have walked one hour and it is nearly dark.

I follow Mohammed's stooped figure to where he stops at the bottom of some high rocks where the camels are unloaded. They have begun to shiver slightly in the cold and rain. The Bedu hobble and couch them away from each other, and Hamad goes around with a grain bag. The sacks of grain and equipment are piled together. No attempt is made to find firewood. We await their cue but none comes.

Silently Mohammed hands around half a hard bread roll the size of a fist to each of us. That is our dinner - we really have begun to live as desert nomads.

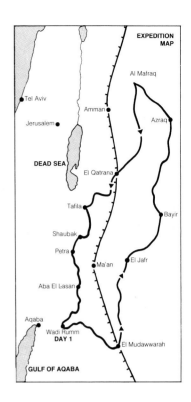

Our bed for the night is a rock ledge with a deep layer of goat droppings. There is a reasonable overhang keeping the drizzle out although the water has begun now to trickle down the rock fissures. The stain on the ground grows darker, each drip of water raising a sigh of dust, and then suddenly its downhill wall breaks, releasing a small river that gathers up the loose particles, floating them along its course. I see it flow by my sleeping bag and watch warily for the next one to form. Our shelter from the elements is approximately 30 feet up a rock incline, with the camels and bulk of the equipment on the desert floor below. James and I lie on our fronts sharing the light of a single torch and begin to write up the diary for the day.

'You'll catch your first fleas from this goat shit,' jokes James as he flicks his kaffiyah to one side in a gesture similar to Mohammed's. I glance around before replying. The expedition members are all sleeping at different angles and intervals along the ledge with the Bedu firmly nestled on grain sacks under a thick covering of blankets. Across the small wadi, the silhouette of the opposing hills stands black and the stretch of sand in between, where the camels are couched, is barely discernible. It has stopped raining but the clouds remain unbroken and foreboding. It's not quite the classic Arabian star-studded sky and 'stories around the campfire' that I expected. The day's entry begins:

'The Bedu are undoubtedly hardy people but I think lazy. Today had I not made a stand we would not have moved on further. There were plenty of excuses about the state of the camels - well, if we can still walk I am sure they can. Perhaps the

Getting used to living with the Bedouin. The second night north of El Mudawwarah. Left to right: James, Hamad, Chris, Mohammed, and Mark.

'The Arabs, who usually lived in heaps, suspected some ulterior reason for any too careful privacy. To remember this, and to foreswear all selfish peace and quiet while wandering with them, was one of the least pleasant lessons of the desert war: and humiliating, too, for it was a part of pride with Englishmen to hug solitude...' Seven Pillars of Wisdom

English mental strength, endurance and adaptability to changing situations is what Lawrence was so respected for by the Bedu.'

I make myself as comfortable as possible. It is a relief to zip up the sleeping bag and retire into one's own shell, shutting out the hunger and doubts of the day.

15 February

'Camel is tired... Camel is hungry,' complains Abdulla opening the morning's conversation.

'Today no go. Him want me stay here,' says Mohammed supporting the issue as he drags a grain sack up the rocky incline. The expedition has barely begun but there is quite clearly a very basic problem. Quite why it exists is beyond the reasoning and imagination of any of us. Nonetheless Mohammed is making it quite clear that the caravan will stay put and all the food and equipment is to be carried to last night's rock ledge. The camels have been tended to by Hamad and now they are tethered to fresh grazing. Most of them tremble in the cold dawn, their eyes vacant and miserable. They look at me with malice as if I dare expect them to carry the loads today. The sky is overcast and the wadi too is drained of colour with its damp sand and the grey brittle camel thorn bushes. The uppermost surfaces of the uneven rocks faintly shine from the drizzle. Disturbed areas of dry sand stand out a lighter shade than the rest and mark the spots where the camels had lain couched during the night. Their forelegs are doubled-up when they kneel, and then tightly hobbled with rope below the joint so as to immobilise them. A high pile of fresh droppings at each end of the dry sand patches show which way the camel had faced; the piles being surprisingly large for the few hours of darkness.

I take in such details as I glance quickly around at the desolate scene. James, Mark and Chris are standing nearby too, which creates the impression (although unintentional) of a unified front. The three Bedu look down on us from the rock ledge and I realise that now is not the moment to stand idle and allow them to dictate the tone or speed of the expedition. Mohammed continues to shout loudly and gesticulate, the general gist of the torrent of Arabic being that bad weather is on the way and therefore we should rest the day. Abdulla whines about the camels again. The echoes of their voices roll across and up the wadi with the sounds wrapping themselves together and wrestling among the crags.

'OK team, let's get organised and make some tea for starters.'

'Sounds like a Hamlet advertisement,' retorts Mark. 'When you have a crisis make a cup of tea!' A thoroughly English move. Soon a good pile of camel thorn twigs, which are not too damp, is collected. I begin to light the fire using pages from my diary as kindling whilst the others find the kettle, tea and sugar.

The tension remains high between the two camps despite my cheerful and positive air, which on the one hand serves to boost my morale and displays at least a modicum of leadership to the team, and on the other shows these strange Bedu that we are unperturbed and determined. I tell the others to begin packing their kit, which is wet from a heavy hailstorm during the night, and to start centralising the remaining sacks of equipment.

Mohammed comes down to the wadi floor pulling his brown robe tightly around his slim frame for extra warmth. I tell him clearly that the weather is good, the camels are good and that today we will travel further towards El Mudawwarah.

'Mister, Captain...Mister,' continues Abdulla who remains tucked under his sheepskin coat on a grain sack in the rock ledge above. I ignore him and direct all my attention to Mohammed, moving closer to him and looking him squarely in the face while repeating my intention to move forward. Something seems to work as he shouts across to Hamad who is now shambling down the rocks with some blankets to join us, muttering to himself as he goes, and intermittently waving his free hand emphatically above his head. I squat by the fire and fan the embers with the bottom of my thobe, half watching and half listening for developments. The kettle has nearly boiled and I measure out three small glasses of sugar to add to it. Suddenly Mohammed is beside me removing the lid of the pot and looking inside. Aggressively he asks whether the sugar is already in the water. When I reply no, he stands up shouting and raving at the top of his voice, and kicks the kettle over. A small cloud of steam is all that remains as the eagerly awaited water is soaked up by the sand.

I do not protest. We are all baffled by the tantrum. The volume of echoing Arabic fills the silent brooding emptiness of the wadi, which absorbs it all with such tolerance.

Then, despite everything and without any of us understanding what has happened or what was said or is being said, a general movement indicates that the caravan will soon be ready to leave. Mohammed and Hamad are kneeling by the camels untying their front legs. Then they are led slowly to where the saddles, blankets and sacks of equipment lie in heaps on the ground. Each camel is couched by pulling down on the head rope, simultaneously tapping the sand directly beneath it and issuing forth guttural 'kh-kh-kh-kh' sounds from the back of the throat. Somewhat timorously and with deep bellows of complaint they flop down onto their forelegs, settle onto their hind knees and then sink onto their hocks. Once down and hobbled the animal is in position for saddling and loading. James has successfully just completed the same performance without any rebuke from Mohammed or the others. Encouraged by the apparent ease with which a camel can be couched I tell Chris and Mark to bring in the two that are grazing farthest away on large bushes higher up the wadi. The saddling and loading phases - noisy and chaotic - come next. The camels stretch their long necks out into the sand. Snarling and belching and roaring they lift their heads up high again, flare their nostrils and stretch the flesh around the teeth to expose them in their cruelest and most threatening light.

On a camel's chest is a circular protruding pad not dissimilar to a fifth hoof that acts as an undercarriage and keeps its belly off the ground. Once the covering of blankets or sacking has formed a protective mould around the hump, it is simply a matter of passing the girth under the animal and firmly securing the riding saddle with a few simple hitches. Each is accompanied in turn by bellows of protest and spitting. As the loads of sacks, water containers, grain bags, cooking utensils and saddle bags are hooped over the saddle pommels I wonder that the incumbent weight does not flatten the animal completely. The procedure of loading is most important, particularly in ensuring the correct balance and the absence of sharp protrusions. Yesterday one of the heavy sacks filled with navigation equipment and weighty travelling bags had rubbed against the rear leg of Chris's camel every time it took a step forward - the skin around the thigh had broken and a large and ugly cut had formed that bled freely, coating the brown sacking with dramatic colour. The camel had developed a limp after a few hours and it surprised me that the Bedu had not paid attention to its plight earlier.

Once a camel is loaded it is not left couched for very long. The rope around the foreleg is untied and with an encouraging 'click-click' from the rider (similar to a 'giddy-up' to a horse) the animal struggles to his feet. A final shake from Hashan to settle his load more comfortably and we are ready. Normally the camel would be mounted while couched, but this morning I suggest we walk for the first two hours out of consideration for the 'cold and tired camels', and because I remembered a line in Thesiger* about it

*Wilfred Patrick Thesiger, CBE, DSO, MA(Oxon), soldier explorer and author of *Arabian Sands* (1959), *The Marsh Arabs* (1964), *Desert, Marsh and Mountain: the world of a nomad* (1979).

Mark rising on his camel.

'A major climax was when I realised the camels weren't as good as I thought they were going to be.'

being good to walk the camels initially, letting them adjust to the loads whilst ridding their bodies of the night's stiffness. After a final look at the map and a bearing of south-east on the Silva compass, I lead off to join the main course of the valley we had come down last night. It is 7.15 am. There is silence. The mountains and desert are ours again and they willingly accept the sovereignty of the caravan as it departs.

Suddenly there is a violent scream from behind. I turn to see Mohammed thrashing his camel wildly across the neck with his stick, his right arm a blur as the blows rain down on the now panic stricken beast. I consider intervening but don't. Mohammed stops and picks up his sandal from the sand - it has a broken strap where the camel had trodden on his foot. He examines it with a disgusted look and begins to beat his bellowing camel again. Obviously satisfied he pulls on the head rope and walks on, barefoot, muttering to himself. These two flarings of temper in such a short space of time are disconcerting, and as I continue I wonder if this morning's performance will be repeated every morning. James raises his eyebrows, echoing my thoughts about our newly acquired travelling companions. There are 985 miles to go.

The wide valley runs south-east and there is little problem in route selection. It is deserted and I admire its ageless beauty as

James rising on his camel.

'Arab processes were clear, Arab minds moved logically as our own, with nothing radically incomprehensible or different, except the premiss.' Seven Pillars of Wisdom

surely as Lawrence must have done when he rode the same way with his Bedouin raiding party. On that occasion he wrote of how he had spent all day riding backwards and forwards between different tribal groups seeking to repair their differences and squabbles, knowing that by El Mudawwarah they must work as one if they were to be successful in the forthcoming action against the Turks. His care had paid off and by the light of tamarisk fires, on the first night, the raiders had formed into only three camps: Lawrence's party, a group of Howeitat and a splinter party with the Bedouin leader, Zaal.

Given the freedom of the sand I stretch my legs as these thoughts come to me, although normal length of stride is partially hindered by our thobes. The kaffiyah forms a comfortable and warming cocoon around the neck and head. After thirty minutes at a steady pace, the sun breaks through and at once the day improves. I turn around to look at our caravan and see Hamad and Abdulla riding at the rear talking with each other. Appro-

41

En route for El Mudawwarah.

'Landscapes, in childhood's dream, were so vast and silent. We looked backward through our memory for the prototype up which all men had walked between such walls toward such an open square as that in front where this road seemed to end...' Seven Pillars of Wisdom

priately the sun clouds over, and I feel a strong sense of betrayal and frustration - their apparent scheming over the state of the camels in order to indulge their idleness is quite evident.

'James, it looks as though our roles will be reversed if we are not careful.' I nod in their direction. James looks up from his thoughts and follows my indignant gaze.

'Yah, they're crafty you know - perhaps we should ride ourselves and not allow them to hold the head rope. The sooner we show our mastery of the camels, the sooner we will be rid of the need for Hamad and Abdulla.'

Being complete masters of our own welfare and of the camels is indeed a high priority. I strongly resent seeing Mohammed walk barefoot leading his camel while the other two 'extras' ride behind. If I did not have the knowledge of Geoffrey Moorhouse's experiences in *A Fearful Void* - his feeling of being the victim in a conspiracy by the Bedu had hindered his goal - I would act more naively to these irregularities.

My thoughts are interrupted by James' camel. The amount of noise it makes when he couches it would suggest that he was pulling it down by the nether regions! Nevertheless he is down, and I turn to Hashan, with an undeserved confidence for my first attempt, and begin to enjoy the 'kh-kh-kh-kh' rasp as I pull down hard on the head rope. Hashan obliges and I am impressed.

Abdulla and Hamad have dismounted by now and come across to us looking anxiously at the camels as if they are couched on beds of nails!

'You ride mister?' inquires Abdulla.

I want to tell him it is a stupid question but my face remains expressionless. He holds Hashan's head close to the ground while I move to the left side of the saddle. Facing rear, left hand on the front pommel for balance, I throw my right leg over and ease myself onto the cushioning sheepskin rugs. I enjoy the sensation of Hashan's apparent struggle to rise and the commanding view achieved from the height of the saddle. As Abdulla leads me off I ask him to allow me the head rope and Mohammed encourages him to do so. James rides ahead on his own, looking at ease with his mount, and soon I am following him, for Hashan is strong. I relish the new-found freedom of control. Behind, Chris and Mark are being led on their camels by Hamad and Mohammed while Abdulla walks alone, to all intents and purposes unemployed.

We ride thus for two hours. Quietly I appraise Hashan from my vantage point, watching the steady rhythm of his head and looking for the first sign of him bolting across the sand. My caution soon disappears. I have a steady and reliable quadruped. Earlier, James had taught me the rudiments of control as Hashan bounded headlong past him in the wrong direction.

'How do you steer these brutes?' I shouted over my shoulder as I shot past him.

'Tap on the left of the neck to go right and right to go left.'

With this worked out I was pleasantly surprised to see Hashan respond with a precision worthy of a thoroughbred competing at Badminton.

The valley begins to narrow into two separate wadis channelling the tide of sand in opposite directions. At that point the tamarisk stands high and Mohammed leads us to it. It is 10 am when he dismounts and we eagerly follow suit. Our concern now is not the distance covered but whether we would be eating anything at this halt. The Bedu are relaxed and smiling. It encourages us to ask questions and clearly they have forgotten the earlier differences of opinion. While the tea is brewing, Hamad takes one of the large tin bowls we purchased in Aqaba and begins filling it with handfuls of flour from the sack.

'Arbood...now you will eat arbood, good,' Abdulla says as he tucks into a bag of small bread rolls. We watch with envy, but are unsure whether the food is his or our own. Nevertheless with the continuing assurances that arbood is good, especially when Hamad makes it, Abdulla feasts himself turning next to the container of olives. Mohammed contentedly smokes a cigarette and prods the fire with his riding stick.

'Hamad chief cook,' I say with a smile.

'Yes,' they applaud with laughter repeating the title. He grins broadly and having added water to the bowl now kneads the dough between his fingers, scooping it together and turning it over and over to crush out the dry pockets of powder.

'Ana,' Mohammed announces pointing to himself, 'Chief.'

Everyone laughs but none more than Mohammed. Sensing a case of mistaken identity I burrow through my Arab/English dictionary to find the word 'guide' which I can add to his statement.

Wind raises the fine dust and sand which whirls around us. Hamad continues to turn the dough that gradually binds its own ingredients, and we watch every move. A tin of Nestles condensed milk is savagely opened with Mohammed's curved knife and its contents added to the tea pot. One glass is poured, returned to the pot, poured again, and then Mohammed

43

carefully places it in front of himself. Six glasses delicately coated in dust and sand remain empty by the fire while Mohammed drinks. Obviously satisfied with the sample, the waiting glasses are filled from a great height, and handed around according to Mohammed's batting order since the distribution does not flow either clockwise or anti-clockwise. A fine layer of sand floats on the surface. Chris puts in a finger to remove it, but the rest of us follow the Bedu example and noisily slurp the hot and refreshingly sweet liquid.

With the kettle removed from the fire the cinders are raked into the sand and flattened down. Hamad shapes the dough into a large pat which he allows to hang until it stretches. No flame remains in the fire, only glowing cinders that flare in the gusts of wind. The pat is dumped on this and covered with sand, cinders and camel dung. We watch fascinated as the dough is completely covered from view. Our first meal is cooking.

Hamad pours water liberally into the bowl to clean it and wash his own hands. The excess use of the precious fluid seems remarkable when a quick scour with sand would have been as effective. He looks up. His bare feet are tucked beneath his robes, and the strangely orange and white kaffiyah hangs loosely. He grins at his own efforts.

'Ques (good)?' he asks watching my face intently.

'Awah, Ham, ques,' I reply and he seems content. Perhaps his eyes are not so shifty after all. We wait. More tea is drunk and the sand continues to cover everything.

Ten minutes later an exploratory removal of the top layer of cinders convinces Mohammed that both colour and consistency are good. The exterior has gone hard and it is the colour of the outside skin of an old stilton. Hamad spreads a dirty piece of sacking to put it on, and he scrapes away with his knife at the foreign bodies of wood and charcoal that adhere.

We look on interested but sceptical.

The bread is broken and then equal sized pieces are handed to each man. It is surprisingly palatable, we conclude, while chewing away like savages, washing it down with tea mixed with sand. If the grit and camel hair is ignored, it is a soft, dry sponge, and just a little filling.

'Ques (good)?'

'Ques...shokran (thank you).'

The others eat more tentatively. It reminds me of being forced to eat cold grey haddock squares - a minefield of bones - at prep school every Thursday lunchtime. The difference is that there the duty master had stood gravely over me long after the other boys had gleefully left, whereas here the sheer necessity to fuel the body against the desert rigours provides the compelling incentive.

'Mumtaaz (excellent).'

I sound both enthusiastic and grateful to Hamad and everyone looks pleased. Slowly, very slowly, the strangeness is disappearing.

It is two hours before the camels are loaded. Mohammed leads off and after another hour the succession of eroded sandstone hills, fallen rocks, tamarisk and shifting sand begins to be left behind. 'Winding downhill in a narrow valley between moderate sandstone walls: till before sunset we were vent on another flat of laid yellow mud,' was how Lawrence had described it.

At around 2.30 pm an isolated pinnacle of rock, the shape of a mushroom, appears directly ahead. The desert is open to either side and less sandy than that eroded from the jebel nearer Rumm. Mohammed begins to head for the leeward side of the outcrop as the wind has begun to blow strongly and is rather cold despite clear sky. We reach its shelter - I had presumed for a brief respite from the elements, but the Bedu begin to unload the camels. Not being exactly sure what is going on I say nothing to them but couch Hashan, remove the sacks, and hand him to Hamad for hobbling.

We've only been moving three hours since the last stop, and if this carries on we will not progress far at all. I understand the camels require to be paced initially, but I begin to feel we are being treated more like American tourists than an army expedition intent on pushing itself to the limit.

The tea things come out, wood is gathered for a fire, the tea ritual is performed, by which time it is getting on for 4 pm. I say nothing - the right moment has to be chosen.

'Captain, sleep here yes?' Of course Abdulla is the first to speak in such matters. I have missed the right moment.

'No, no sleep here.'

It's a familiar phrase.

'Mohammed, still two hours more light...we go,' I say to him in a mixture of English and Arabic.

'Not good, Mohammed, we must quickly, quickly. Tomorrow Mudawwarah,' I go on.

'Mundawarrah-ha,' Hamad corrects me with a smile, missing my tone of voice. In fact all three of them seem perfectly happy. I begin to see that this is their normal routine and speed, and that my aims are completely beyond their comprehension.

'Look mister,' begins Abdulla again in his sickly voice. 'You must slowly, slowly for camels. Camels is hungry.'

'Mohammed,' I plead, 'camel is good. We must go two hours then sleep!' He looks at me sizing up this nuisance that has so recently muddled his leisurely life. I feel I have pressed him too far.

Abdulla squats and picks his teeth with loud, distracting sucking noises. Hamad absent-mindedly prods at the dead cinders in the fire with his stick. I continue to look at Mohammed for a decision as he reclines against his saddle bags smoking. His eyes are bright and sharp as they stare me through. It is a tense moment. With one hand he wipes his face with the end of his kaffiyah which he tucks into the black rope band on his head. He gives an indifferent shrug of the shoulders, speaks to the others and then stands up.

When he shouts at Abdulla to retrieve the camel that, despite being hobbled, has wandered further than the others, I know that we have won a minor victory.

After an hour we notice a sandstorm in the distance. It comes on us quickly, and we wrap our kaffiyahs tightly over our faces leaving only small vision slits. Looking at everyone dressed thus with the wind forcing their robes against the outline of their bodies, the loose material flapping at the rear, I feel a tinge of excitement. Everything in the desert is exciting to the beginner. My ankles and hands are exposed and they come under constant bombardment from tiny grains. A layer is deposited particle by particle in the fold of my kaffiyah directly beneath my eyes, and I squint to see even 50 metres ahead.

'Kayf haalak (How are you) Mohammed?' I shout to him in a muffled voice.

'If all goes well with you then all is well with me, thanks be to God,' he replies having lowered his kaffiyah. The accompanying grin reinforces my suspicion that he might actually be enjoying it.

'Kayf halaak Hamad?'

'Ques, al-Humdoolillah.' (Good, thanks be to God.)

Only Abdulla fails to return a cheerful response. He alone is riding, his partially concealed face bearing his discomfort with reluctant resignation.

When the stinging around my ankles ceases I know we are out of it, though it is difficult to judge in the failing light. The cold wind persists. We climb a small rise and Mohammed sends Hamad to scout ahead for a suitable shelter for sleep, and he rides off to check the high ground on our left while we push on ahead. The pace is good and only one camel, the small female (nagar), shows signs of tiring.

'Bukra (tomorrow) Mudawwarah?' I question Mohammed.

'Awah, bukra Mudawwarah...in shaa Allah.'

'In shaa Allah.'

With barely sufficient light by which to see, we come across a rock buttress similar to the one where we had halted earlier. We unload the camels on the sheltered side and they stand patient and brooding among the loose fallen rocks. In the darkness it is difficult to find our sleeping things, and the sacks have to be closely examined by torchlight.

We discover that all the equipment we put aside as surplus to requirement, including the bivviy bags, had nonetheless been packed by Mohammed and not left behind. Since the night is becoming very cold the others gratefully seize their 'bonus' shelters and begin to clear a space to peg them in. It seems fortunate that these things became mixed up at Wadi Rumm after all.

The evening meal is milkless tea and a couple of hard sticks of bread that Mohammed produces from a dirty bag. They are excellent for dunking but remain a struggle to eat for all that. The fire does not blaze once the kettle has boiled as there is scarcely any wood, and soon we lose that source of heat.

'Torch, where torch?' demands Abdulla. Chris reluctantly hands his black rubber one over. It is another feature of Abdulla that has begun to annoy us. Both last night and so far this evening, he has been incapable of doing anything without a torch, even looking at the fire to see if it is burning well, and he never turns it off. There is adequate light to pour the tea but Abdulla must have a torch. He lays it on the sand with the beam shining into the distance. Chris looks furious but says nothing.

Instead I point to the torch and show Abdulla the 'off' button. My limited Arabic does not extend to explaining that batteries run low and we have only a limited supply for the month. Emulating the Bedu we slurp our tea noisily - Mark occasionally slurps his very loudly as a tease, but they do not notice. In our native clothes, hunched around the lee of the rock with no lights, we could be a band of brigands.

By 7.30 pm everyone is bedded down, and the light from two bivvy bags tells me that Chris and James are writing their diaries. Mohammed works away at levelling off a cavity of sand between two small rock outcrops that will make a protected and snug sleeping area. Turning round he touches my arm and motions me towards it. Thanking him sincerely I pick up my sleeping bag and settle it down while Mohammed puts a large rock at the bottom to prevent me from sliding out.

The generosity and unselfishness of this simple act touches me deeply. I feel very small. By torchlight I read through my diary entry for the day. It ends: 'MM made me a comfortable bed of rock and sand and I feel guilty. The camels are couched and sleep with us. The sky has cleared and it is a beautiful night with only the sound of the wind on the rock face.'

16 February

The camel had remained couched in the same place all night. A stream of green and brown liquid flows down the incline from a reservoir formed around the camel's rear. The smell is appalling and I notice it has dried over the animal's legs in places, forming a glue with the grey sand. The sun is not yet risen. A bleak and uninviting dawn: hunger gnaws in my aching stomach and my mouth waters to a distracting degree. Matted hair, dirty face and hands, sand in every crevice and a gentle rise in body odour are features of our awakening to this dawn. Disregarding the lack of water, I wet my handkerchief and wipe the grime away, using the kaffiyah as a towel.

Mohammed has a fire going with the blackened kettle on top. It looks like an antiquated family heirloom worth many camp fire stories, but it was brand new from the bazaar in Aqaba only three days previously.

Breakfast is sweet tea, no milk, and a couple of the sticks of bread which have an off-putting smell. Very much in need of something other than the tea and bread of the past two days I search out the container of black olives. Abdulla immediately scoops his hand in before I have a chance to offer them around. The others try one each, but are not enthusiastic. I chide them for being too fussy and 'Westernised' at a time when they have little choice.

As we pack to leave I break open one of the many tins of high concentrate glucose tablets that are the basis of our survival rations. Surreptitiously one sweet is given to each man other than the Bedu. In a conversation earlier we had been genuinely concerned by the lack of food. I therefore decided that if this was to persist for a month, no matter how strong or determined we might be, there would be serious problems. We had only been in the country six days and had allowed no time for acclimatisation, let alone such a radical change of diet and life-style. I decided it would be better to build up our reserves of strength now than risk not making the grade later.

Our handlers do not appear too concerned over the wretched state of the camel with dysentery. With a great deal of difficulty they force him to his shaky feet. Long neck outstretched and unblinking eyes staring ahead, he seems oblivious to the stream of fluid flowing down his hind legs. The amount of discharge is staggering.

The distribution of loads is different this morning. The nagar and the sick camel hardly carry a thing, and the heaviest pack goes on 'Barmey' who has become our favourite. He is the split-lipped one who had first held our attention at Wadi Rumm. He earned his affectionate name by his antics with his tongue every time he goes near the nagar, and the squeaking noise he makes as he exhales. He is also the biggest and the strongest.

It is a pitiful looking caravan that heads south-east on its third day across an increasingly barren desert. The sun is up early and by 8 am we begin to feel the heat. The nagar and sick camel are being dragged along at the rear. I wince each time Abdulla beats the sick one, forcing him to greater efforts. Sometimes he stops completely and stands expressionless. With 960 miles to go I fear the worst.

Map reading is awkward and I estimate we are in one of two places when, at 10 am, the party halts for a cigarette. We are either 10 or 20 miles from El Mudawwarah. It is difficult to be more precise than that.

Since Mohammed knows the way it is not a cause for immediate concern - the worry will come later when we travel ground unfamiliar to him. I have learnt already that distance means nothing to the Bedu, and the routes are talked of only in terms of time. El Mudawwarah, for example, was quoted as two maybe three days. God willing of course.

By midday we have travelled, less the halt, for four hours, of which two have been spent riding. I noticed the speed with which the others took the opportunity to ride when, after walking for two hours, I said they could do so. A lack of energy and a touch of light-headedness is certainly the feeling, plus persistent pangs of hunger.

The consistency of the desert begins to change from a sea of small rocks crested with little waves of brown sand, to a more yellow sand speckled with tiny rust coloured stones. When it drifts against a tufted shrub it becomes almost white and clean in texture. Rounding a blackened hill of rock we sight two palm trees and some high tamarisk. It is the nearest to an oasis we have seen. Against the crest of the hill behind it with two redoubts of rocks, horizontally scoured by the erosion of strata, it makes a proud setting spoilt only by the track marks of a vehicle.

'One hour Mudawwarah,' says Mohammed.

'In shaa Allah,' I reply and he nods appreciatively. He then tells me that the area of the palms was an ancient spring and there was a Turkish camp there. Fortunately I remember the Arabic for gun because of its strange pronunciation, and so Mohammed's gesticulating actions of Auda Abu Tayi* killing many Turkish soldiers makes some sense. With 'El Aurens', of course, I interrupt to remind him of the British contribution.

I translate for the others and they take more interest in the ground, looking over it, almost hoping to find a cartridge case, tunic button or cap badge. The desert yields none of its secrets.

A magnificent plain of yellow sand stretches to the horizon as we crest the rise to look south towards Saudi Arabia. Our caravan swings off to the east though, following the line of higher ground until we pass a small desert fort surrounded by palm trees on the high ground half a mile to the left. Mohammed says it is Turkish but Mark prefers it to be a scene from *Beau Geste*.

A few hundred metres further on Mohammed stoops down and picks something off the sand. He stops my camel and hands it to me saying that it is Roman pottery. I study it closely recalling my three mis-spent years at university studying archaeology. Indeed it is Roman, and now Mohammed is handing up several more sherds. I dismount to walk beside him as he tells the history of Jordan in a mixture of Arabic and pidgin English.

'Before Roman came Nabutaean; before Turkey came Roman; Turkey go...English come; English go...Jordan come.'

It is not so much a grasp of history by an uneducated desert tribesman who can neither read nor write that impresses me, but his identification of the Roman pottery. Talking it over with James we decide that features of the desert and related stories must be passed down through generation after generation by campfire talk and travels along the ancient trade routes.

Walking becomes difficult as the sand is deep and soft, long

*Lawrence met Auda in April 1917, and together they mounted a series of attacks on the Turks (including blowing up the rails of the Hejaz railway at Wadi Deraa in May) which led up to the final assault on Aqaba, and made Lawrence's reputation. Auda Abu Tayi was described by Lawrence as the 'master type' of the Howeitat tribe, the Toweiha under him as 'the first fighters of the desert'.

dunes that are tipped with a coarse and spiky grass. Mohammed points out what looks like an old water tower and a building that is El Mudawwarah.

I was expecting a village of mud-walled houses and noisy bazaars at least, perhaps with a place to buy a cold drink and somewhere to supplement our meagre rations.

Yet the elation of having the goal of the expedition's first leg in sight surpasses all thoughts of personal comfort. The others push ahead. Even the two poorly camels have settled into a better rhythm, and I stand on a dune to take a photograph. Mohammed stops 100 metres ahead and waits. When I reach him he points out some bones in the sand that are bleached white and look very old. He tells me that they are Turkish dead killed when the Bedu attacked El Mudawwarah with Lawrence, during the Arab Revolt*.

I remain sceptical and push on, yet a sense of history immediately strikes me when I get my first glimpse over the next rise. There lies the twisted remains of the Hejaz railway that was such an important feature of the Revolt and Lawrence's actions in it. I look hard for the train but see nothing other than railway debris. To the left I can see the old Turkish railway station that Lawrence had 'recced' the night before blowing the line further south. Suddenly I realise that he must have looked at it from a similar position to the approach route we are making... 'In front and below lay the station, its doors and windows sharply marked by the yellow cooking fires and lights of the garrison...Zaal and I crawled across the last flat, till we could count the unlighted tents and hear the men talking. One came out a few steps in our direction, then hesitated. He struck a match to light a cigarette, and the bold light flooded his face, so that we saw him plainly, a young, hollow-faced sickly officer.'

Except for the absence of tents the picture might well have been similar. Certainly the few nondescript buildings look old and derelict enough, except for one which I assume is the desert police post.

I stand holding the rein of Hashan and take in the scene. A bright red and yellow juggernaut passes over a fly-over above the old railway half a mile away that I had not seen. The illusion dissolves.

---

*Subsequent correspondence with Mr Rory Moore MBE (ex-captain Imperial Camel Corps) has established that in fact the site where the remains were found coincides with the position of Turkish sangars he drew on a map: he was present when, after a fierce fight, the garrison finally fell to the ICC in August 1918. Lawrence was not present at the action, although he assisted Colonel Buxton with his reconnaissance.

Chapter Three

My skin glows and I shiver slightly with the stark contrast, for the room is almost cold after the intensity of the sun. Inside the Desert Police Post at El Mudawwarah, surroundings that are familiar but strange to us all at once, we become self-conscious. The strangeness of chairs, a cleanly swept floor, and sweet tea which arrives free from the lingering expectation and effort required to boil a kettle on a brushwood fire. These small luxuries have an immediate impact, since nearly three days of camels, desert and Bedouin life have educated us already in the requirements of the long journey. But it seems more than that. Even in this short time our Westernised attitudes have changed and we have adapted to a different life. Small things like our peeling noses, the burn marks on our thobes from the fires, and the Arabic way in which we slurp our tea, make us feel more travelled and integrated than we really are. I register these thoughts and others as the shadows of the walls confine us in temporary protective relief from the harshness outside.

The morning journey had been hot and tiring, and El Mudawwarah shimmered in colourless lines as we made our final approach over deep sand. The camels were couched and left as a car might be, parked opposite the police post under the harsh sun, for there was no shade. I wondered at the lack of fuss being made over the animals' obvious needs, and am fearful for the consequences of their slowness on the success of the expedition.

The occasional lorry rumbles past the police post on the road connecting Jordan's southernmost border with Saudi Arabia. I had immediately resented the intrusion on the traditional Bedouin life-style into which we have 'escaped'. The lorry drivers were the first we had seen since Wadi Rumm, and suddenly our desert privacy mattered strongly to us. I realised then that it was a false dream, a naive plan, and a touch romantic for me to have supposed the desert might still be a sanctuary. During the overall planning of the expedition I had conveniently ignored the thin red lines on the maps depicting roads, vaguely assuming that they would not affect us. Yet the roads are there, and we can no longer ignore them.

The lorries use their horns noisily, and the Arab drivers look at the camels as though seeing them for the first time in their lives. For their part the camels lie quietly chewing on their regurgitated food with absent-minded indifference. They maintain an aura of dignity amid this technological invasion, and our Bedouin exude a similar dignity as they greet the police. It is as if suddenly two different worlds meet. As I watch Mohammed and Hamad I see the grace and humility of desert tribesman to best advantage.

Sitting now in the police chief's office, our party is very much the centre of interest and speculation. On the dirty whitewashed walls a handsome portrait of King Hussein stares down at everyone, the only decoration in a room which is otherwise bare and devoid of any status. There are no books, no telephone, no files on the dusty desk. In the conventional sense of the word it could hardly be described as an office: were the walls to be substituted by a goat-hair tent the effect would be the same, and in every way there remains in this room an intangible tribal feeling.

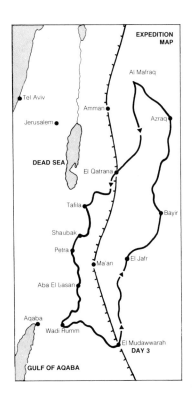

Now the expedition is at El Mudawwarah, the most important thing is to reach the wreckage of the train that Lawrence blew up at Hallat Ammar in 1917. It is a personal goal, as well as a promise to Tom Beaumont, and I am impatient to find it. To pose for photographs on our camels beside its remains will be a fitting commemoration to Lawrence's memory. It will satisfy our sponsors too. 'How far Lawrence's train?' I ask the man in a soiled green uniform behind the desk. There are no badges of rank or unit insignia on his clothes. He raises his eyebrows for a moment and frowns, continuing to regard me from behind a blue cloud of cigarette smoke which drifts at one level across the room. With an abrupt jut of his chin in Mohammed's direction he searches for some meaning and clarification.

'What you want?' Mohammed asks of me in a tone that is almost edgy because I have interrupted his own line of conversation with the other Arabs. 'Lawrence's train, how many hours from here?' There is still confusion. I expected it to be a well known local feature and within an easy ride of the police post. Ever since we had been seated in the room I had searched the desert horizon through the rusty open windows, hoping to interpret something from the scattered and tangled remains of the old Hejaz line. 'Is it here?' 'What?' 'The train...Turkish soldier...guns... Auda Abu Tayi and El Aurens.' I put as many Arabic words together as possible to build the picture which I emphasise with child-like 'choo-choo' noises. They still appear not to understand. My mention of Auda's name distracts Mohammed, and causes him to launch into what can only be a flowing discourse on the birth of the Jordanian nation, and of how it is the journeys and actions of the great desert lion Auda that we are following. Lawrence is not mentioned. I find the long and roundabout way of achieving anything with the Bedu increasingly frustrating.

Silent spectators to it all, we sit in a line watching and listening, quietly drinking our tea. I think of the train. It is an obsession, and such a vital part of the meaning of our entire venture. If we were to reach it soon I would be happy that one of our major goals had been achieved. At least it would be something to show for all the planning and all our efforts. Yet at the back of my mind I know the problem is compounded by the state of two of the camels. I cannot understand how they can be so obviously ill after only such a short time. With our collective lack of Arabic and knowledge of the people, I begin to feel a little at sea amongst it all.

The Arabs in the room are talking even more loudly than before, and I know I must bide my time and allow Mohammed to do things his way with his own people. It is as if we do not exist in the small room, and for the first time I feel that our disguise in Bedouin clothing is a mockery to these Arabs. In an attempt to conceal my growing unease I pick up the copy of *Seven Pillars of Wisdom* from my photographic bag, and begin to read again Lawrence's own account of the raid on the railway line which led to the destruction of the Turkish troop train...

It was at dawn on 19 September, 1917, that Lawrence rode further south of the railway station at El Mudawwarah. The previous night's recce with Zaal had convinced him that their numbers were insufficient to engage the Turks there. In the safety of an anonymous desert the raiding party selected an area of high ground overlooking a bridge on the railway line. The Mudawwarah garrison of two hundred troops now lay 15 miles to the north, and 4 miles south was a further Turkish base, the hillpost at Hallat Ammar. It took Lawrence two hours to dig in the charges on the track. A further three hours were spent concealing the stiff wires running from the detonator in the explosives to the firing point - this was in the hills overlooking the ambush area. It went well until at sunset a party of the Bedouin accidently skylined themselves and were fired upon by the Turks at Hallat Ammar. Obviously suspicious, the Turks despatched a hundred troops from Mudawwarah in the morning to follow up the sighting. Lawrence watched their approach through his binoculars and was faced with a difficult decision - either stay and hope to remain undetected, or leave the charge in place and return later in the hope that the soldiers would not notice it, or pack everything away and disappear into the desert. As it was he decided to leave the charge and move the Bedouin away from the area. Just as this was happening a sentry spotted the smoke from a train heading north from Hallat Ammar towards the ambush. Lawrence yelled at his Arabs to get into position, and his two British sergeants manned their machine guns - both men were suffering from dysentery after drinking from the well near Mudawwarah, which the Turks had polluted with dead camels.

The train came into view and Lawrence noted the two locomotives were pulling carriages full of troops. He decided to give the signal to the young Arab Salem, who would press the plunger at the firing point, at the moment the second train was on the bridge.

'There followed a terrific roar, and the line vanished from sight behind a spouting column of black dust and smoke...the hollow was alive with shots, and with the brown figures of the Bedouin leaping forward to grips with the enemy...our machine guns chattered over my head, and the long rows of Turks on the carriage roofs rolled over, and were swept off the top like bales of cotton before the furious shower of bullets which stormed along the roofs and splashed clouds of yellow chips from the planking...'

The surviving Turks took cover behind a ridge and began returning fire, but they were effectively neutralised by Sergeant Stokes' mortar. His rounds fell well and the Turks fled in confusion, presenting themselves as ideal targets to the machine gunners...' The sergeant grimly traversed with drum after drum, till the open sand was littered with bodies.'

Lawrence ran to the track to inspect the damage, noting that the first wagon had fallen into the space where the bridge had been and that the carriage was filled with sick men: 'The smash had killed all but three or four and had rolled dead and dying into a bleeding heap against the splintered end. One of those yet alive deliriously cried out the word typhus. So I wedged shut the door, and left them there, alone.'

Oblivious to the buzz of conversation in the room, I sit captivated by the bloody and passionate account of the action. My mind fills with vivid pictures, and my heart races with the anticipation of actually going to the train to see it first-hand. At the same time I am gloomily aware of the more pressing problem of the camels. I fear that if Mohammed does make a strong case for resting them, admittedly the proper course, we will be delayed for a few days. He might even decide to return to Wadi Rumm for fresher and stronger camels, one of two options he spoke of on the way to the police post.

The problem is made greater by the long route north-east from El Mudawwarah to our next destination, El Jafr, a journey of some 85 miles across an empty desert - not one water hole is marked on the map.

Mohammed is still talking. The man behind the desk is also a Howeitat, and despite being familiar with the greatness of Auda, he clearly enjoys Mohammed's story as though hearing it for the first time. Hamad and Abdulla sit on the floor with their backs to the wall saying nothing, allowing Mohammed mastery of the situation, so it seems. A young man wearing green fatigues and 'flip flops' squats in the centre of the room, washing small glasses in a tin bowl and occasionally stopping to listen. He interjects and says something which starts a three-way conversation. Another policeman arrives, and after offering the traditional greetings to everyone, he remains leaning on the door in the sunlight. Then when he too joins in, they turn to look at him, and the conversation goes four ways.

I look at my watch and realise that in the last forty minutes we are no further towards solving the problem of our mounts, or finding the whereabouts of the train, than when crossing the burning hot sand earlier in the day. A frustration promoted by the language barrier and the strange working of the Arab mind begins to rise in me.

'Mohammed, who is police chief?' I ask searching for some authority in the ocean of Bedouin timelessness and flexibility. Mohammed stops talking and nods to the man behind the desk - who this time beams a smile in return. I produce my Arabic dictionary and struggle through it to select the opening words to the queries I have isolated.

'Chief, he want know where you go?' Mohammed asks as though aware of my thoughts.

'From here?'

'Awah.' (Yes.)

'El Jafer,' I say, pleased at last to be talking about something of relevance to our movements.

'Jafr....ra,' corrects Hamad with a smile, and for the first time he talks loudly and authoritatively while pointing in the rough direction of north.

Remembering our safe passes with the marked route and explanation, I take mine from the back of my diary and hand it across the desk. The Arab serving the tea and the other by the doorway immediately move behind the chief's chair to study this new development. All three of them examine it minutely and grin as they translate our names, looking up to see which one of us responds. When Selley becomes 'silly' it is our turn to laugh and the atmosphere relaxes a little. Another man enters the room, greets us, and joins the gathering who by now are stabbing at the map with their fingers, and talking quickly and excitedly as is their way.

'Mister, why you do this?' the new arrival asks on looking up from the map.

'You speak English?' I ask in a glimmer of hope.

'A little...a little.'

I explain in simple terms. He appears to understand and translates it for the others. They look at us with incredulity, as if wondering why any sane man would wish to ride 1,000 miles across their desert when there are some perfectly serviceable Toyota pick-ups available. I notice Mohammed smiles at this, as though for the first time taking pride in his undertaking.

I ask the English speaker about the train, and he says it lies in completely the opposite direction to El Jafr, nearly 15 miles due south by some low hills. At our present speed I calculate it is a day's distance but the detour will mean a two-day journey even before halts are taken into account or the plight of the camels is considered. I feel trapped and frustrated. I still cannot conceive how the camels can be so poor, or why it appears that other desert travellers I had studied would seem to average 20 miles a day at least. Lawrence sometimes wrote of covering 50. There again I reassure myself that our expedition took the same time from Wadi Rumm to El Mudawwarah that Lawrence had taken back in September 1917.

I establish that there are three camels Mohammed is unhappy about. He wishes to leave the worst two at the police post rather than risk them dying in the desert. His replies appear tired and disinterested now that the real problems are being addressed, and he repeats over and over again that if I was to speak to Brigadier Shobaky everything would be solved. There is no telephone, and I begin to appreciate that there will be no quick solution to it all.

'You must slowly, slowly with the camels,' the policeman implores me. Mohammed looks away, and I know the implication is that we are pushing not only the camels too hard but also the handlers. The realisation is alarming, and the implication for the future, disheartening. I had presumed that we were dealing with tribesmen and animals who are among the hardiest in the world, but now I realise I had not counted on the motivation factor and the Bedouin's different perceptions of time and daily speed.

'Mohammed are there camels at Jafr?' I ask seeking a further option.

'Yimkin (Perhaps). How many camels you want go Jafr...three, four, six?'

I look hard and coldly at him, barely understanding why he does not advise me or take the initiative himself and decide what is the best solution - it is his desert, his tribe and he has lived with camels all his life. His apparent unwillingness to lead even in his own field of expertise is irritating and wasteful. It reminds me of a similar but more significant frustration that Lawrence felt in Wadi Rumm shortly before the raid near El Mudawwarah: 'Poor Sherif Aid's uselessness, even as a nominal leader, forced me to assume the direction myself, against both principle and judgement; since the special arts of tribal raiding and the details of the food-halts and pasturage, road-direction, pay, disputes, division of spoils, feuds and march order were much outside the syllabus of the Oxford School of History.'

I know it is a crucial decision, but I feel sadly lacking in all the facts: I know that the sickest camels will not reach the train and then turn about at once and cover the near 100 miles to El Jafr; I also know that returning to Rumm for fresh camels is unthinkable, and leaving the two sickest at Mudawwarah is to jeopardise our safe crossing of the Jafr plain. With only one month to complete the route it is a continual race against time. Finally, the need to keep the camels alive for the entire journey and the lack of funds to purchase any replacements dictates my decision. With a feeling of failure I reluctantly decide to head directly to El Jafr.

'Mohammed, six camels go Jafr today,' I state firmly.

'Mister, sleep here, camel need rest...tomorrow go Jafr,' Abdulla immediately and predictably says before Mohammed can react to my decision. Hamad says nothing and merely stares at his bare feet with a concerned frown. The room is silent, Mohammed looks at me with a tired and negative expression. A buzz of conversation develops among the Arabs - none of which I

Above: 'Mohammed was aristocratic, uncouth, beautiful, ugly, generous, selfish...and it was this extraordinary man who really taught me so much of desert life.'

Above right: *Hamad cooks our first meal.*

Right: 'Suddenly one of the camels leans his head back, and simultaneously a large pink tongue, alive and slobbering, spills from the left side of his mouth, almost a foot long. The camel's head shakes. The pinkness fills with air causing different areas to inflate and deflate in ripples - each expansion accompanied by a deep gurgling that sounds like the repulsive intermittent snoring of a dirty old man.'

Left: *'We cross the Hejaz railway... For two years Lawrence lived and dressed as an Arab, endured great hardship and assumed a responsibility which resulted in him being the focal direction of the Revolt. He led raids by camel against the Hejaz railway behind enemy lines and blew up a number of Turkish trains: the railway was the strategic and logistical link on which the success of the Revolt became virtually dependant; without it, the Turkish garrisons were isolated and vulnerable to attack from the army of irregular Bedouin... My immediate impression is how difficult it must have been to bury an explosive charge and conceal its wires. It is completely exposed all round.'*

Above left: *The approach to El Jafr across the salt flats - Lawrence first entered Jafr in April, 1917, with an army of some 500 Bedu, and it was from this place that the final operation to capture Aqaba (which helped make his reputation) was later mounted.*
Lawrence wrote: *'Dawn in Jefer (sic) came imperceptibly through the mist like a ghost of sunlight, which left the earth untouched, and demonstrated itself as a glittering blink against the eyes alone. Things at their heads stood matt against the pearl-grey horizon, and at their feet melted softly into the ground. Our shadows had no edge: we doubted if that faint stain upon the soil below was cast by us or not.'*

Above right: *En route from Bayir to Azraq, Lawrence's headquarters in the winter of 1917, 'we reach a small wadi covered in delicate white and purple wild flowers. Fragile, they hide among thorn clusters and behind small boulders, yet still cannot escape the feverish search of hungry camels, who devour this luxurious grazing like desert hoovers.'*

The expedition reached El Jafr at 8 pm on 19 February, some sixty-eight years later.

Above: *Thlaithukhwat.*
*'We, ourselves, felt tiny in
it, and our urgent progress
across its immensity was a
stillness or immobility of
futile effort.'* Seven Pillars
of Wisdom

Left: *Azraq Castle, just
visible in background, where
the expedition stayed the
night:* *'Azraq lay
favourably for us, and the
old fort would be convenient
headquarters if we made it
habitable, no matter how
severe the winter...'*
Seven Pillars of Wisdom

understand.

'Mister, I think you sleep here, tomorrow you rest and maybe in one or two days you go Jafr...in shaa Allah,' says the English-speaking policeman. Everyone turns to look at me. Mohammed assumes an air of casual neutrality and stares out of the window.

'That's just bloody stupid,' remarks James in a rare outburst of emotion. Mark chuckles and Chris continues to write his diary. The Arabs seem to pick up on the tone of James' remark and are silent again, as though awaiting further clarification. The room is hot and stifling all of a sudden, and I am irritated by an itching rash on the tops of my hands. I am impatient to leave now that I have made the decision to try and reach El Jafr with all the camels. It is an impatience fuelled by the desire to turn my back on our failure to reach the train, and the instinct that once away from the other Arabs my own handlers will be more responsive to my will. I know that to halt will be fatal to the timings of the expedition, and I would rather return to the desert and rest the camels there.

'No! No sleep here. Today go Jafr,' I reply emphatically, my feelings stoically defensive after assuming the responsibility for an alien situation. As one, they turn to Mohammed. He observes me in a gentle, forgiving way.

'Yimkin...in shaa Allah,' (Perhaps...God willing,) he mutters quietly.

'If I hear those words again, James, I'll go mad.'

'It's their philosophy.'

It appears my decision is accepted, and only Abdulla looks sulky - I am beginning to loathe him. He leaves the room with Hamad to feed the camels, and with them go three of the others. Mohammed and the police chief remain. Thankfully we are no longer the centre of attention and I feel relieved at the prospect of retreating into the privacy of the desert once more.

Hamad returns with our large cooking bowls. He stands in the doorway, a simple and obedient expression on his face, and Mohammed curtly says something to him. Hamad mumbles his reply and appears clumsy beside the almost aristocratic Mohammed. I notice the poorer quality of Hamad's clothing, his darker skin, and the ridiculously large and battered plimsolls he has just put on - the toes of his right foot are protruding. He wears a faded brown jacket over his robes and his kaffiyah is a filthy orange colour. Their differences have gone unobserved until now.

Despite my anger with Mohammed's apathetic approach to the problem with the camels, I feel reassured by his commanding presence when I compare him with Hamad or any of the Bedouins we have met. There is a great tease in his smile and daring in his laugh, and having observed the reverence with which the others listened to him earlier, I realise he must be a known and respected member of the Howeitat.

'I went native this morning,' says James, interrupting my thoughts, 'and used a rounded stone instead of toilet paper.'

'What was it like?'

'Not recommended,' he replies with a wry smile. We laugh and feel happier for the opportunity to do so after the constant heckling over the camels.

Hamad leaves and Mohammed informs us that the policemen have invited us to eat a mensaff with them. We are delighted at the prospect after two and a half days with virtually no food. Mark reclines further in his chair and loudly describes his choicest dishes, the flowing descriptions promoting our now familiar hunger pangs and feeling of light-headedness. At this point Chris quietly informs us that he did not enjoy the mensaff in Wadi Rumm because he is a vegetarian.

'Well you'll be pushed to find any vegetables and fresh fruit in this desert,' jokes Mark. Although we tease him and dismiss it light-heartedly I am annoyed about this sudden revelation, and silently wonder how he will adapt to the desert life and diet as the expedition really gets going.

As we wait for the food I ponder again the decision that I have reached, agonising over it in my mind, and trying in some ways to justify it and in others to search for alternatives. There are none if the expedition is to maintain its schedule.

Due to the last-minute change of plan following the cancellation of the original 1,000-mile journey through Saudi Arabia, our research and preparations (especially in terms of topographic information about our present route) are inadequate for decision-making purposes. Even so, there was no reason to suppose that the camels would let us down so early.

Not seeing the train is a bitter blow.

I pick up Lawrence's book again to distract myself from these many inward-looking thoughts. I study closely the picture of him in native dress, thinking myself into him, and wondering at the exact nature of the man: the complicated intellect, the charisma which attracted people, the romantic and the visionary, the chivalrous knight in the desert, and the extraordinary vulnerability of the post-war Lawrence, the subsequent architect of his own enigma and the pursuing legend which inwardly destroyed him.

I turn to the haunting dedicatory poem at the beginning of the book, and try to analyse the ambiguity of its meaning...*

I loved you, so I drew these tides of men into my hands and wrote
    my will across the sky in stars
To earn you Freedom, the seven-pillared worthy house, that your
    eyes might be shining for me
                      When we came.

*The poem was dedicated by Lawrence to S.A. Some say the letters refer to Sheik Achmed, the nickname of Lawrence's boy servant and intimate friend, Dahoum. Others have suggested they refer to Saudi Arabia. As with much else in *Seven Pillars*, there is no certain view.

Death seemed my servant on the road, till we were near and saw
    you waiting:
When you smiled, and in sorrowful envy he outran me and took
    you apart:

                      Into his quietness.

Love, the way-weary, groped to your body, our brief wage ours
    for the moment
Before earth's soft hand explored your shape, and the blind
    worms grew fat upon

                      Your substance.

Men prayed me that I set our work, the inviolate house, as a
    memory of you.
But for fit monument I shattered it, unfinished: and now
The little things creep out to patch themselves hovels
    in the marred shadow

                      Of your gift.

The reading of it is refreshing and it relaxes my mind. I am stirred
by its depth and beauty as well as by the complexities of its
hidden meaning. Lawrence seems to challenge his reader to
interpret clues, and in so doing offers a small key with which to
open the door to his mind, an insight to his personality.

My brief solitude of thought is interrupted by Mohammed. He
calls my name and points to the book on my lap. I tell him it is
about El Aurens and Auda Abu Tayi and how they fought the
Turkish. Immediately his face lights up and he moves across to
squat beside me. He is fascinated by the picture of Lawrence and
examines it minutely while nodding his head in admiration as
though he knew the man. When he sees the picture of Auda he
beams proudly, and excitedly takes the book to show the man at
the desk. Simultaneously two men walking past the door outside
are called in and soon they are crowding around the pictures with
touching reverence. Eagerly I watch their reaction to Lawrence.
It is one of acceptance and understanding - who he was, his
name, and his role in fighting the Turkish. But it is the picture of
Auda which stirs them most. The book has an obvious impact
upon them all, and the fact that we are carrying a picture of the
famous Howeitat leader suddenly brings our party more closely
to them. Their appreciative smiles and obvious pleasure is touching. Mohammed hands the book back as if it were now a sacred
item. I notice too how he would not allow anyone else to hold it.

'This man's son, the son of Auda, is living in El Jafr. You will
meet with him,' explains the English speaker. This is something
we did not know until that moment; the information is exciting:
the son of Auda, who himself fought with Lawrence in later
battles, is now a grand old man in his eighties and living at our
next major stopping point!

Suddenly I am filled with a new sense of purpose. The train

was a known goal, but now we have the unexpected opportunity to retrace the Lawrence legend through the Abu Tayi at El Jafr.

I had never dreamt of actually finding here anyone still alive who had known Lawrence, and it was beyond my wildest hopes to meet someone who was so closely involved in the Revolt. Auda's son is mentioned in *Seven Pillars of Wisdom*. He was only a boy of eleven years when Lawrence met him, but a boy of that age is considered a man in the world of the Bedouin.

I am mindful that the unique opportunity might have been missed without the chance showing of the book and Auda's picture, and it takes me away from my depressing thoughts of the train. I look at the Bedu opposite through different eyes and wonder at the strength of Howeitat tribal history and how much they might teach us through passed down stories of Lawrence and Auda Abu Tayi.

Instead of feeling the expedition has lost something by its setbacks, I feel what we might gain by a growing affinity with the Bedouin. In mood the venture changes from a journey of endurance into one of reliving Lawrence through the Bedouin of today. I realise for the first time our privileged position and suddenly am conscious of the real nature of our journey - the opportunity to learn first-hand with the benefit of time afforded us by the gentle speed of our chosen mode of transport.

'Yallah! Yallah!' shouts Mohammed once the camels have been loaded. It is 4.30 pm. The glare and heat of the sun remind us of the barrenness of our venture - the naked exposure of ourselves to the elements. Some ten men from the police post come to watch the caravan's departure. They stand and smile, cheerful and talkative, with their hands either in their pockets or around the arm of a friend. It is the first time Chris and Mark have seen such familiarity and I am amused to watch their reaction for a while. Then I tell them it is quite natural among the Arabs and they look even more surprised.

'Rope!' shouts Mohammed next, which we have learnt is his executive command to unhobble the head rope from around the forelock of the leg. Obediently we bend to do this, conscious of the looks and laughter of the other Arabs who remain fascinated by our Englishness and the incongruous manner of our travel.

The route is to the north-east and directly across the Jafr plain. Mohammed has calculated it will take us four days, 'in shaa Allah'. Apart from the crate of oranges given to us at Mudawwarah, our food stocks remain the same. The absence of further nourishment concerns me, especially considering the sparse diet up until now. The mensaff at the police post had been badly needed and we devoured it quickly, oblivious to Arab etiquette of leaving sufficient for one's hosts in the second sitting. Mohammed became annoyed and rebuked us for the greed shown by our innocent intentions. Nevertheless we are strengthened by the meal and the reserve of energy it will give us to counter the harshness of the coming days.

With our backs to the sun we walk the camels north. The landscape is vast and flat, and the horizon appears constant in its distance to us - unblemished and empty. This void engulfs us both in its physical size and in the uncertainty of survival in its wilderness. We cross the Hejaz railway which itself looks incongruous as its precise lines cut through the desert. My immediate impression is how difficult it must have been to bury an explosive charge and conceal its wires. It is completely exposed all round.

For the first time I appreciate the problems of remaining undetected in a desert war, and the skill and cunning behind Lawrence's raids. After tours in Northern Ireland I understand the requirements for a terrorist ambush, but there the advantages of abundant foliage and camouflage assist the terrorist in surprising the security forces. In the desert there is nothing, and it makes the success of Lawrence's raid on the line to the south more creditable in my own eyes. Once more I regret the decision over the train and hate the pressure that time forces on us.

There are 950 miles to go.

Chris Selley and Abdulla. The cylindrical case is 'the lurid orange tripod' on which is mounted the theodolite.

'The landscape is vast and flat, and the horizon appears constant in its distance to us - unblemished and empty.'

The pace is slow, our progress dictated by the nagar camel who is becoming weaker by the hour. She carries barely any of the expedition supplies yet still Abdulla has to drag her along behind the others. After three hours I estimate only 5 miles to have been covered, and this increases my uncertainty of the wisdom in pushing on ahead despite the advice of the Bedu. Mohammed walks alone at the front as though to force the pace and prove me wrong. It is obvious the two sick camels need to halt the night, but it has been dark for an hour and Mohammed still continues, stubbornly pulling his camel onwards and ignoring the plight of the sick ones. I check the compass bearing, straining to interpret clearly the luminous needle which wavers from side to side as I walk.

Navigation under such circumstances is a little imprecise since there is no fixed point on the ground to head for. In addition, the map of the desert to El Jafr lacks any detailed information or main navigational features, apart from the Jebel Ratyeh, and I am aware of the serious implications of our somewhat hit-and-miss approach.

Using a combination of the compass bearing from Mudawwarah and the time and distance equation, it is possible to establish a rough or 'dead-reckoning' position on the ground, and I tell James he will need to confirm this accurately with a star-fix when we halt. We have difficulty walking over the uneven desert in the darkness - it's nearly impossible to pick out or predict the small ankle-turning undulations. Mohammed declares that the camels should not be ridden; it seems that the night-sight of camels is also poor, and Hashan occasionally stumbles or halts as though afraid to commit his hooves to the ground.

It turns colder. We trudge along tiredly, the night silent apart from the sound of a gentle wind around my kaffiyah and the sloshing of the water carriers on Hashan. I am content to continue for as long as Mohammed is willing to push the pace of the camels. Each hour is a few miles covered, and each mile is one step closer to El Jafr where it may be possible to get fresh camels from the Abu Tayi.

Finally Mohammed stops in a small hollow offering a break from the increasing wind. Under the canopy of a multitude of stars we couch and hobble the camels on sharp desert stones - as they settle they bellow in a unison of complaint, and the loaded sacks are unhooked from the saddles.

Mohammed had gathered some isolated camel thorn before dusk while walking along, and now he directs us to search for more. We fumble blindly for the scraggly bushes, stubbing the toes of our feet on many hidden obstacles. In the darkness our soft hands are cut and splintered as obstinate roots refuse to yield their brittle off-shoots, and all the time Mohammed rests against the grain sacks, his cigarette glowing, and the small fire of his brushwood lit before him. I smile and realise what a wily old devil he is. One by one we return with the contributions of our foraging efforts to sit around the fire. The cherished kettle is filled with water, the sugar is added, and the sack of tea strategically placed beside the sandy glasses. The Arabian sweet-tea ritual is the focal point of our day's end.

Hamad is tending the camels, feeding each with a nose bag and ensuring they are securely hobbled for the night. Abdulla squats beside us noisily eating an orange.

'Typical of him to get his paws in first,' groans Chris. Abdulla finishes and wipes his hands on the end of his kaffiyah. Next he hawks and sniffs with impressive gusto before projecting a large lump of phlegm onto the sand between his feet.

'I think I'd better distribute these oranges before "young roaming gums" eats them all,' I say looking at Abdulla. He beams in response, not understanding the nature of my gripe.

When the tea is made I take a glass to James. He stands silhouetted against the magnificent pale evening sky. The tripod is set up and the mini-theodolite secured. He scans the stars to identify the three needed for a fix. There appear to be more and more each time I try to identify one from the chart, which we pore over by torchlight.

The chart shows the main stars to be seen in the northern hemisphere, and the identification of them is made simpler by the constellations. We identify the Plough first - seven stars in the shape of a saucepan - and then the North or Pole star. The others can then be read off from the chart. The theodolite measures a bearing to each in turn, which is computed with the exact time and related to the Nautical Almanac tables.

The tables provide the stars' exact position for each second of the year. The final calculation is made and the three bearings of the stars drawn on a map, inward to the spot of the observer on the ground. The resulting triangle thus pinpoints the observer's position. The mathematics involved in the calculations are beyond me, and, as at Aqaba, I study the lines and columns of figures as though they were Egyptian hieroglyphics.

I stand shivering in the cold. The wind blows steadily and the landscape seems dead beneath the sparkling sky. I can just see the shadows of camels in the depression and occasional red sparks whipped up by the wind from the dying embers of the fire. James hands me two watches set to GMT and Jordanian time. I'm to record the nearest second the moment he takes a fix.

James blows on his hands and rubs them together. He flicks his kaffiyah to one side and squints through the theodolite eyepiece. Carefully he adjusts its position onto the approach line of the star Regulus. He checks the bubbles are centred and appears satisfied.

I contemplate the ridiculousness of the scene - two men standing in the desert not 10 miles from civilisation, taking star shots.

I record the time and readings that James gives me from the theodolite. We complete the three stars in half an hour and return thankfully into the protection of the hollow, out of the wind. The others are asleep on the stony ground. I place some of the few remaining twigs on the fire to warm my hands and feet. It flares and fades quickly. Beside me James sits with a small torch in his mouth, working diligently on his calculations. The equations completed he draws the lines in on the map which should cross to form a triangle within which we are sitting now.

Our navigational skills may not be vitally important to our safety at this point, but this first test will serve as a useful trial run for the expanse of Jafr plain and the northern areas which Mohammed will not know.

'Looks promising,' James says as he draws the first line.

'Where are we then?'

I am silent as he draws the second, knowing how crucial his skill might be later in the journey.

'You won't believe this.'

'Try me.'

'We're in the middle of the Dead Sea.'

Chapter Four

17 February

Before us, the scene is uninviting: empty desert, a void as far as the eye can see, shimmering silently under layers of heat. Only our small caravan appears to exist; it adds shades of living, moving colour to the otherwise blue and brown divide. Our surroundings absorb our passage as though it never occurred.

The imprint of a human foot or camel hoof is as ephemeral as the passing shadows of man and animal that drift by. Their shade covers the sand from eternal exposure for a fleeting second, and then they are gone forever.

The caravan halts beside a sparse clump of brushwood. It is 11 am, and the expedition has moved continuously since 6.30. The progress has been good despite the two weak camels, and I estimate approximately 9 miles have been covered. At dawn our departure had been without the usual revitalising drink of tea to ease the cold of the new day. There was nothing with which to make the fire and the routine was sorely missed. Though we no longer dwell on the absence of food before the noon-day halt, nevertheless our hunger persists and the relief of halting is now heightened by the sight of Hamad preparing bread.

We watch as he busily kneads the flour and water together in a dirty tin bowl. It is small and rusty and Chris says that he wouldn't feed his dog from such a vessel. Mohammed leans forward to set the kettle in the hottest area of the fire. Quickly he snatches his hand away from the invisible flames and uses his riding stick instead. He doesn't look at me but concentrates on not spilling the precious brew.

'Where is the large bowl?' I ask, remembering not having seen it or any other cooking equipment in the sack hanging from Barmey's saddle.

'Give to Police,' he replies nonchalantly. The fact that it had been bought as expedition equipment in Aqaba seems immaterial to him and this annoys me. It also reminds me of his oversight about the water supplies at Wadi Rumm. I learn the Arab mind slowly.

Just as the tea is poured a sudden wind whips up small clouds of sand. The fine particles swirl around the huddled group, covering everything in a delicate coating.

'Absolutely typical,' groans Chris as he puts a finger in to scoop floating bits from his tea. We hold a protective hand over the tops of our glasses and turn our backs to the wind. The clouds of dust virtually obliterate the horizon, and nothing escapes the

Left to right: *Mark, Hamad, Abdulla, Mohammed, Chris, and James.*

'We hold a protective hand over the tops of our glasses and turn our backs to the wind.'

impact of it all - every crevice, every fold in our clothing is affected. Unperturbed, Hamad continues to make the arbood and disregards the amount of sand which the congealed mass attracts with each new gust of wind. Finally, he places it among the embers of the fire to bake. We eye our main meal with enthusiasm, trying to avoid comparisons with Western food and knowing we must eat anything available if we are to preserve our strength.

As we wait, Abdulla opens the plastic container of olives. He takes a handful and leaves the lid on the ground. We watch as he spits out each stone and takes a couple more,and still the container remains open to the swirling sand.

'You'd think living in the desert would make him better trained,' comments James as he reaches over to replace the lid.

'Yah, well look now at Hamad, and I thought water was an important consideration,' I reply and nod to where Hamad is cleaning the tin bowl: he fills it from the jerry-can and washes the congealed lumps of flour from it; the dirty water is emptied and the bowl rinsed for a second time; finally he uses his left hand as a cup to pour water into, and with great deliberation he washes his face, arms and hands. The spilt water is absorbed within seconds and only dark stains remain.

I ask Hamad why the bowl cannot be cleaned with sand. He replies that there is plenty of water in the desert, and besides, the sand is unclean. The logic of this escapes me and runs contrary to survival training that I had received earlier in my army career. I regret not having stopped him earlier. As travellers of the desert the Bedu have everything to teach us, but in other respects common sense must prevail. I remind myself of the dangers of merely observing and not leading the expedition. As Lawrence wrote 'The Bedu are odd people. For an Englishman, sojourning with them was unsatisfactory unless he had the patience wide and deep as the sea.'

When it is ready, Mohammed breaks the bread, handing us each a piece as we sit huddled together to form a shield against the worst of the sand. Like a benevolent father he fills our eagerly outstretched hands. Despite the camel hairs, sand and lumps of charcoal, the unappetising bread is ravenously consumed. It's all there is, and strangely it is all we want.

We move again at 12.30 pm. The wind persists, tearing at loose clothing, ripping into our bodies and trying our remaining vestiges of patience. In single file, leading the camels on foot, our grimly determined party continues across the desert. No one talks. Each man either stares at the ground immediately in front or studies the rear of the camel he follows.

I walk behind Abdulla's camel and the strong odour and green sticky fluid running down its hind legs convinces me of its miserable state. The blown sand sticks to its clogged fur and the poor animal walks with an awkward rhythm. Except for lightening the load the Bedu have done nothing to relieve its deteriorating condition. I appreciate that in pushing on to El Jafr I may be signing its death warrant. The Bedu, on the other hand, appear resigned to this fact and drag the suffering beast along as if to get the maximum mileage before it keels over.

In truth, remembering how Geoffrey Moorhouse lost two camels on his Sahara expedition, I feel nothing for this one's fate and accept it as one of the expedition hazards. Somewhat selfishly the thought of returning home with tales of disease and dead camels in the desert even holds some appeal.

By late afternoon we are in poor shape. James and I both feel tired and light-headed, and Mohammed limps badly from a troublesome ankle. The camels look worn, and their unco-operative behaviour is proof of this - occasionally one of the weaker ones crashes to the ground bellowing his complaint, which is the surest sign they require a rest. For five hours a steady pace has been maintained, all the time battling into the increasingly ferocious wind with thousands of sand particles stinging our exposed flesh. Ahead is the Jebel Ratyeh. The low hill juts into the plain, and it is the only major feature en route to Jafr. I look at it with relief as the high ground means cover from the sandstorm, yet the distorted shape appears no closer as we trudge silently towards it, bent and wrapped against the wind, the camels aloof and staring ahead with their shining eyes, mirrors of moisture.

A small wadi with softer sand, clumps of tamarisk and brush-wood meanders into the jebel. We reach the foothills through the wadi's outlet and halt gratefully behind the lee of the rock. On the surface of the tapering fingers of sand the particles dance, fighting the wind to remain on their ridges. There is utter silence away from the elements.

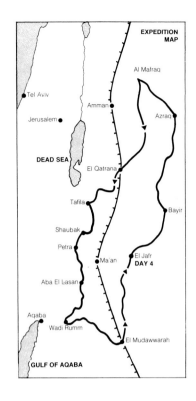

We eagerly begin the routine of establishing camp. It is the first halt made in the light hours, and allows us the opportunity to busy ourselves with personal concerns. Methodically, each man sets up his bivviy bag and clears a sleeping area. Tamarisk is collected in abundant quantities for the fire, daily diaries are updated and the map is marked with the route and an accurate grid reference of our position obtained. Equipment is cleaned of sand, the photograph log is carefully recorded, and attention is paid to personal hygiene. It is glorious to rest, a rare chance to care about nothing and indulge ourselves. Usually the hours spent not travelling are equally arduous, for it is the continual challenge for existence and survival in a nomadic world without push-button technology.

Suddenly the peace is interrupted by the snarling and painful bellowing of a distressed animal. I look to see our Bedu around a camel lying on its side and struggling with fear and rage. Abdulla has his hand over its nostrils forcing the camel's head on the ground. Hamad is kneeling on a hind leg pulling on its tail. Mohammed stands poised with a red hot piece of metal I had seen him place in the fire earlier. The victim of this rough handling is the camel with dysentery. The two camels tethered nearby look on with dumb sympathy - their small ears flick sideways, backwards and forwards like sensitive radars locating their companion's distress calls. Mohammed lowers the poker onto the top lip of the camel's mouth. Smoke rises and flesh burns. The animal screams in pain, its tongue whipping in and out as quickly as a snake, the lips pulling tightly over the teeth forcing them outwards in a deathly skeletal display.

Abdulla strengthens his hold and forces two fingers up its nostrils, pulling them away from the head and downwards. Mohammed returns to the fire with the poker. When it is hot again he moves to the rear of the frightened animal whose eyes stare wide and white with terror. I grimace as Mohammed

A camel with dysentery about to be cured in the best Bedouin fashion.

'Hamad is kneeling on a hind leg, pulling on its tail. Mohammed stands poised with a red hot piece of metal I had seen him place in the fire earlier.'

applies the poker to the area around the rectum, and the camel fairly rises off the ground in shock. The ropes stretch to breaking point and the Bedu tighten their holds to restrain its writhing body. Gradually the high-pitched screams die down. Satisfied, they release their grip and untie its legs. The animal struggles quickly to its feet and shakes the dirt from its fur. There are no outward signs of emotion, and the extraordinary expression of the camel is as though nothing had happened.

'I'll tell you what,' says Mark, 'there's no way Mohammed will know if I catch dysentery.'

'I can just imagine him chasing you across the sand brandishing his red hot poker,' chortles Chris. Much discussion and speculation follows the incident, all of which is a welcome change after the day's drudgery.

I remind myself that Lawrence rarely mentioned having any trouble with his camels. He always rode a female racing camel for its staying power and ease of control. I still do not understand why we are riding bulls when most desert explorers write about their being better as baggage animals. The need to carry out such rudimentary medicine on one of our own mounts worries me, particularly because any further set-backs will seriously affect our success. The camels Lawrence rode were of the finest, and if a problem arose he was in a position to change his mount easily.

Around the fire, later in the evening, there is a feeling of closer companionship with the Bedu. Mohammed cries with laughter at our expressions of fear that he might seek to remedy one of our own illnesses with a poker. He wears a bandage on his swollen ankle with shy pride after Chris had tended to him. Morale is high, a fact partly due to the long halt, but mainly because we have eaten the first evening meal of the journey. Hamad had baked bread and Mohammed had produced a battered tin of sardines between seven of us. By the standards of the last four days it had been a feast.

Only Abdulla remains outside our circle. He complains less frequently now, although his weary-looking face betrays his immaturity. He is clearly experiencing difficulty in maintaining this harsh life away from the Bedouin camps. It is a revealing insight into a society noted for its children assuming adult responsibilities at a very young age. It is considered normal for an Arab boy aged about ten to be left alone to tend a herd of goats in the desert. This rapid disappearance of childhood accounts for Auda Abu Tayi's son, aged only eleven or twelve, accompanying him in skirmishes against the Turks. Western children, by comparison, remain protected by the gradual transition from childhood to manhood. Abdulla it seems is caught somewhere between the two.

18 February

It is the hour for the routine morning halt. Despite the intense heat the sweet tea is refreshing. Everyone is lethargic and even the camels look hot, their yellow and green spittle has dried and hangs about their mouths as proof of their exertions. We have only about five pints of water left for seven men with still 40 miles to El Jafr.

The dawn wind had been cold and it had been with much reluctance that I got out of the warmth of my sleeping bag to dress. The camels were loaded, and after some bread scraps and tea we moved off. First there was the Jebel Ratyeh to ascend, about 800 to 1,000 feet, and this we did in a tight caravan winding our way up over large boulders. It took more than an hour to reach the top and we struggled slowly over rugged desert of flints and small rocks. There was no wind, and it was hard and monotonous work making our way over the wadis until, eventually, we hit the plain again. I have never seen anything so flat - an unending flint plain whose image was distorted by the haze of heat. There was silence as we rode on, gently swaying in motion with the camels. Our kaffiyahs kept the heat off and we were thankful for that. As I rode I could hear little except for Hashan's feet striking the ground, and the noise of splashing water from the two jerry-cans hanging from my saddle. I was furious when James confessed the jerry-cans had not been refilled completely at Mudawwarah due to the angle of the tap on the wall. I was more furious still after Hamad's display yesterday and when Abdulla admitted to having had a leaking container all morning.

Now the midday heat is oppressive and the glare from the sun quite blinding, but we elect to keep moving. The camels are mounted in silence and the caravan departs. Chris has cramp in his legs and decides to walk in order to ease it. We agree that we must be mad. The flat plain of black flint desert stretches for miles and miles, not a single feature and no other humans; yet we continue to head roughly north-east on a compass bearing, launching ourselves across it all with hardly a drop of water.

'Mad dogs and Englishmen,' jokes James.

'You're right. Even the map has nothing marked in its 10 kilometre square grids except "Desert Grave" in the odd place,' I reply.

'Vaguely reassuring.'

I watch James as he smiles and draws on the last of a cigarette. The motion of his camel is gentle and flowing: he sits side-saddle, his left leg around the front pommel and hanging over the grain sacks at the side. The reins are in his left hand, and in his right a riding stick which he taps at intervals on the camel's neck for speed and direction. He appears confident and seasoned in his mastery of the style and art of riding. He had his own camel while a member of the Multi National Monitoring Force in the Sinai two months earlier, much to the amazement of the American contingent in particular.

Mark however maintains a nervous posture. He does not enjoy being perched so high above the ground in a swaying saddle over

18 February. *The ascent of Jebel Ratyeh (about 800 to 1,000 feet).*

'There was no wind, and it was hard and monotonous work, making our way over the wadis until, eventually, we hit the plain again.'

which he has no control. His snub nose is bright red and peeling, the rest of him a vulnerable lily-white. He lacks poise and is as awkward in motion as is his camel. He has lost his riding stick but nevertheless prefers to hang on to the front pommel with both hands. It is an amusing sight.

Chris strides confidently beside us. The sleeves of his thobe are rolled up and already his arms are quite brown. Around his waist is his camel's hobbling rope which adds a little body-shape to the otherwise cumbersome appearance of the thobe. He wears sandals, and with his springing step he gives the impression of a neat person who is content with his lot. He is a strong walker and is obviously unaffected by the oppressive heat.

I tentatively direct Hashan to ride beside Mark so that I can talk to him. The camels draw level but come too close. Their loads clash and they snarl at each other, bucking their hind legs and plunging their long necks forward. Mark ends up hanging half in and half out of the saddle. Barmey halts, looking perplexed, and Mark jumps down and decides to keep his feet on the ground. He picks up a small pebble, pops it in his mouth, pulls hard on the rein, and resolutely walks on. I ask him what the pebble is for.

'Stops you getting thirsty,' he replies. 'You suck on it and it keeps your saliva going.' He takes it out and holds it up for me to see. I feel my own cracked lips and chuckle, remarking to him that it may be a good Scout trick but it exaggerates our predicament a little. At the back of my mind is a worry that the real danger in our situation is that we may be unable to find our way out of the area once the water has been drunk.

After three hours the desert changes slightly, the flattened black flint giving way to a looser sandy texture. We move through a line of dead trees and bushes, a dried stream bed, and evidence of old Bedu campfires with occasional bleached animal bones lying around. It is 5 pm. We long to halt but cannot afford the time. I stop to study the map. James joins me and we take the opportunity to pause for a smoke break. The others sit down and allow the camels to graze on the sparse bushes.

'Where are we?' he asks as the map is spread on the sand. I point to a minute patch of green specks, the only data besides a thin contour line in the entire grid square. I take a bearing with the Silva compass to the police post marked at El Jafr.

We move off once more, and wearily the remainder follow, some riding but most walking. It is hard going in the heat and monotony of the plain. Mohammed branches off at a tangent and the others follow him automatically.

'Mohammed, where you go?' I ask and point in the direction the compass indicates.

'Boosalla mush ques,' (Compass not good,) he scoffs. He turns his back and walks on assuming he is right. The others look to me for a decision, unsure whether to follow Mohammed or myself. Again I feel he is eroding my leadership of the party and I lose my temper. Handing James the rein of my camel I run after Mohammed to resolve the issue.

'Which way you go?' he asks fiercely jabbing a finger at my chest when I reach him. While spreading the map I realise it is the first time I have explained how it all works. I point to our position, to El Jafr and work through how the bearing is found. Mohammed studies the map intently but I realise it is meaningless to him. He stands up.

'Mohammed good,' he says tapping his head with one finger. He points to the sun, the shadows from his nose, his body and small stones, and indicates that he knows where to go.

'Boosalla mush ques,' he repeats with a dismissive flick of his hand. He moves off leaving me standing alone and unsure, working out the angle of our differing routes. Then instinct tells me not to fight their ways and arrogantly insist on leading in the conventional sense.

Small comfort is derived from the near continual battle that I recall Moorhouse had with his handlers over the route. In a restrained sulk I walk at the rear, impatiently checking the increasing swing of the compass needle away from where I think we should be heading. I decide to give Mohammed his first chance to prove his navigation beyond doubt.

Dusk comes quickly. I had tackled Mohammed twice about the direction, each time increasing the hostility between us. Now I barely restrain my frustration that we may have travelled five hours in a wrong direction while nearly out of water. Having allowed him the benfit of the doubt I lack the patience to see it through. A severe headache, sore eyes from the glare, and a dirty sweaty feeling does not improve my temper. The camel with dysentery walks slowly in front. The fur has dried hard around its legs which is a favourable sign, and it has kept good pace throughout the day. Droves of flies feed on the filth, and the persistent smell is exaggerated by the heat.

The discomfort of the sun, lack of water, the strangeness of the Bedu language and ways, makes this the worst part of the journey so far. We are tired and irritable, unsettled by the anticipation of further problems and only too aware of our aching physical condition. Now I really appreciate the trials Lawrence endured, and more particularly how he did so as a foreigner alone for so much of it. At least the burden of our suffering is lightened by a common bond of language and the shared challenges of the new life-style.

'Is that a tent?' asks Mark, turning to me and pointing to our left. I strain my eyes to interpret the distant shadows in the fading light.

'Mohammed...Bedu?' I query hopefully. A tent means water, people mean shelter and food, Bedouin mean advice on the direction of Jafr, I think as I await Mohammed's reply. He sits on his carefully controlled mount and sweeps the area with the binoculars. I had produced them earlier in the day to assist navigation and immediately Mohammed had wanted them to claim the distinction of chief guide as well as chief handler. Now he uses them as though a professional field commander. I realise that because he likes them he means to keep them; it's the Arab way. The lightweight Zeiss binoculars belong to my brother, but now that they are in Mohammed's hands I will have to accept that they will not be leaving Jordan.

Mark's sighting does indeed prove to be a tent, and gleefully we head towards it. Conversation is revived and all thoughts of perishing in the wilderness are dismissed. When we finally reach it, we are disappointed to find no one there except for the odd bleating goat roaming around.

'Could put that one in the pot,' chuckles Mark. There is an upright oil barrel half filled with water near one of the tent's guy-ropes. The nagar sniffs it and begins to drink. Mohammed screams in fury and beats the innocent animal with his stick. She backs away, recoiling her neck and bellowing in short pitiful moans. His aggression alarms me and I am uncertain whether it is due to the animal drinking another man's water or his wanting the animal to go for a longer stretch before watering.

Near the black goat-hair tent is a small gulley with the odd clump of camel thorn. It becomes our welcome halting place for the day. The camp routine carries on in the gathering dark, and water is brought from the drum by Abdulla. We barely have the energy or enthusiasm to do more than forage for brushwood, and then sit in exhausted huddles by the fire.

In contrast to yesterday's wind, which sapped our energy and left us feeling battered, the breathless air and intense sun has today drained our bodies of fluid and burnt our faces. There is no escape from these exposures, and all the time exists the need to cover just that extra mile to maintain the schedule. It is a degree of hardship in which each of us finds enjoyment, in different ways.

In the darkness we hear the sound of a vehicle, and suddenly pitching shafts of light cut through the black anonymity of our surroundings. Despite any earlier feelings we resent this unexpected visit. The vehicle, a Toyota pick-up, careers to a halt in a choking cloud of dust beside us. A smiling Bedouin gets out and warmly embraces Mohammed, Hamad and, lastly, Abdulla. Tea is poured for the visitor, everyone squats around the fire, and the Bedu talk excitedly together as though enjoying an old reunion of friendship.

'This man,' Mohammed says, patting the shoulder of the new arrival, 'is father to Abdulla.' We look at Abdulla who smiles warmly in return. His father owns the tent.

'Looks far too nice to be his old man,' says Chris, and we laugh at this private joke.

I study Mohammed with renewed interest and respect. There is little doubt he had known his way here, and this meeting is no chance event. Since Mudawwarah he had wandered consistently away from my chosen bearing and it had caused many heated arguments between us: today's events led to the final show-down between us, a clash of personality which had been promised for days. Mohammed carries it lightly. There is no animosity, only generosity and warm fatherly smiles. Again he has made me realise how little I know of him and his way of life.

Abdulla's father leaves. A fire glows in the tent on the higher ground behind us and all the noises of food being prepared, babies, chickens and goats are secure sounds and welcome to us in our nomadic existence. I wonder where they have appeared from, at the same time hoping we might be entertained to a huge feast by Abdulla's father. I am disappointed. Surprisingly Abdulla remains with us. The absence of hospitality is perplexing.

Instead, Hamad bakes bread in the fire. When ready it is broken into the tin bowl, and water is added. We watch the new technique. He produces a dirty sand covered jar of olive oil, some of which is poured into the mixture. The smell is an appalling one of vomit. We wrinkle our noses as Hamad squeezes it - like someone trying to grip a handful of porridge. When it is done he licks his fingers, smiles and places the bowl between us all.

'Welcome,' Mohammed says and gestures to the meal. There is hesitation all round. James, Mark and Chris all look at me for reassurance.

'Mumtaaz (excellent) Hamad,' I coo with feigned delight as slowly I work a handful around my mouth, trying to ignore the smell and at the same time searching for the courage to swallow it. Imitating the Bedouin, I allow my sticky hand to hang limply over my knee near the bowl, and look indifferent at the prospect of eating any more. The others hesitantly dip their hands in the gooey mess, squeeze it into a lump and reluctantly begin to eat.

'Being a vegetarian won't help you now, Chris,' I chuckle as I watch him trying to conceal his disgust. Despite our hunger the meal is revolting. We pretend to enjoy it and the Bedu look pleased. James warns against showing too much false bravado or it will be the main meal every day.

The ordeal over, we sit under a canopy of stars, three Bedouin and four Englishmen, slowly learning about each other and communicating more openly. The story of Mohammed with his poker makes them laugh for the second night in a row. Mohammed heats sand in the fire and applies it to his problem ankle, apparently preferring this old remedy to Chris's bandages and creams. He tells us that tomorrow, God willing, we reach El Jafr. Warmed with this knowledge and drained by the day's exertions, we retire to the sleeping bags early - it is 7.30 pm.

Abruptly disturbed, I struggle out of the oblivion of a deep sleep and look at my watch to discover it is midnight. I lie in the dark cover of the bivvy bag and listen: stern Arab voices, one vehicle - now two, doors slamming and gruff commands. I open a slit in the hood. Against the stars, lit by the brilliance of the moon, stand men in uniforms carrying weapons. Their two landrovers with pintle mounted machine guns look incongruous parked beside the camels. From under the pile of blankets on the grain bags, Mohammed emerges in a humble, confused manner and this does not give me much confidence. It is a strange situation and as I contemplate it a torchlight blinds me. I hear Mohammed's voice beside it, and see the silhouette of an Armalite barrel and a large pair of boots in front of my face. Feeling small and clumsy, I disentangle myself nervously from the folds of the sleeping bag and bivvy bag and stand shivering in the cold night air. The shadow of the man near me asks a question in Arabic which I don't understand. Mohammed explains and I search for my pass and hand it over.

'Kaptan?' asks the voice behind the torch beam. My eyes adjust to the light and I make out that he too is an officer. The torch is lowered and a young lieutenant looks at me, the skin of his face shining in a reflection of the moonlight. He surveys the overall scene: the camels and the sleeping forms of the others. He nods, shakes my hand and tells me his name among other things. Much of it is lost to my sleepy and confused mind. I remain uncertain of the circumstances behind the visit. He leaves and the landrovers start up, their headlights pierce the blackness, and the figures wrapped in heavy coats and kaffiyahs huddle in the rear in sinister array. I am too tired and cold to question Mohammed. As I drift off to sleep again I wonder how they found us in the middle of the desert at midnight, where they came from and, more important, why.

19 February

The first time Lawrence arrived in El Jafr was 30 April, 1917, when he was with an army of some five hundred Bedu. They had travelled from Wejh in Saudi Arabia through the Hejaz mountains to capture Aqaba from the rear. The final operation was triggered from Jafr. Here too lay Auda's camp and the Abu Tayi of the Howeitat tribe were concentrated in the area. As the campaign gained success and pushed the Turks north to Damascus, Emir Feisal came from Saudi and had his headquarters at Jafr in August 1918. Lawrence met him there, arriving himself by aircraft from nearby Guweira. Jafr became a frequent halt for him as he shuttled between Azraq, a headquarters in the north, and Aqaba, the main supply base and port to the south.

On 12 August, 1918, Lawrence used the extra mobility of a Rolls Royce armoured car to 'run out to Jefer* to meet the

---

*El Jafr is the modern spelling. Lawrence explained his own spelling of places in the Preface to *Seven Pillars of Wisdom:* 'Arabic names won't go into English, exactly, for their consonants are not the same as ours, and their vowels, like ours, vary from district to district. There are some "scientific systems" of transliteration, helpful to people who know enough Arabic not to need helping, but a washout for the world. I spell my names anyhow to show what rot the systems are.'

victorious Camel Corps, who came gliding, in splendid trim and formal appearance, across the shining flat just before sunset, officers and men delighted at their Mudowwara success.' The Imperial Camel Corps had finally captured the railway station at El Mudawwarah three days earlier, and then had ridden direct to Jafr. Ever since Lawrence's reconnaissance and raid on the railway line by Hallat Ammar on 19 September, 1917, it had remained a small Turkish outpost behind the advancing allied army.

It has been a long day, frustrating and amusing by turns. Soon after dawn we watered the camels from a desert well near the tent of Abdulla's father - their first drink for five days. During the noon halt Abdulla was caught eating two oranges stolen from the food bag. He squatted with his back towards us at a distance, but the pile of peel was obvious when he returned. It was the first case of deliberate deceit and selfish behaviour among our handlers. Mohammed said nothing. To him oranges are woman's food and not for Bedouin to eat.

Shortly afterwards Abdulla's father appeared in his Toyota pick-up. It had taken him fifteen minutes to cover what had taken us five hours; we no longer felt inaccessible. Our annoyance at this interference with the style of our journey was short-lived - it was worth every second of seeing Abdulla climb into the vehicle and leave us. There were many derogatory remarks as he drove off. Before he had left, his father had tapped his stomach and talked of Abdulla. I interpreted this to mean that his son was ill, and replied abruptly, in Arabic, the equivalent of 'not good' and 'bad.' In fact he meant that Abdulla was his son, 'of the same body', and was most offended by my verdict of his son's worth. However we felt that my interpretation was closer to the truth.

Relieved of the continual whinings of 'Mister, mister,' the sulky figure dragging his feet at the rear, the surreptitious meals he so selfishly relished, and his interference with the camels, the morale of the English contingent soared. It plunged dramatically when, an hour before darkness, a cloud of dust heralded the arrival of a vehicle from Jafr.

Much to our digust Abdulla rejoined the party, talked of promised mensaffs, and, thoroughly refreshed, marched ahead as though he had walked every inch of the way with us. When a sick camel refused to gallop over the salt flats, he dragged it viciously and beat the long suffering animal with a stick. My temper finally snapped with this behaviour and his patronising mockery of everything we stood for. I shouted at him furiously and barely restrained myself from hitting him.

We reached El Jafr at 8 pm after two hours stumbling in the darkness over the marsh grass and small dunes. The radio mast of the police post, sighted four hours previously had prompted expectations of a mensaff which proved unfounded: the expanse of the Jafr salt flats acted like an optical illusion and by dusk the mast appeared to us, in our fatigued state, to be the same distance away.

Thus did the satisfaction of another goal, successfully achieved, fade. The camels stumbled, tempers were lost, the party became separated in the dark, and Mohammed's camel went lame. Completely exhausted, hungry and thirsty, we eventually unloaded the camels by a ruined building near the police station. It had been a gruelling journey.

Now, two and a half hours later, James and I sit wearily amid the smoky chaos inside the Jafr police station. Behind the desk facing the throng is Second Lieutenant Khader Al-Zuher aged twenty-four and commander of the Jafr Police post. Except for Abdulla he is probably the youngest in the room. I count the number of people - there are eighteen, some sitting and some standing, most of them smoking. They wear variously coloured robes, some with worn jackets or coats lined with sheep's wool. White kaffiyahs contrast with red flecked ones. The more eminent men wear black shoes, others have sandals, while the rest go barefoot. Their faces vary from seasoned bark, tinged with grey stubble, to round and olive complexions. They are all Arabs who shout, gesticulate and haggle at once - words are a passion to them and the delivery of them, an art... I admire the Lieutenant's control of the large gathering and they in turn, despite his youth, listen respectfully when he speaks.

Mohammed sits to one side, once again the centre of controversy and debate. The problem is the old one. Mohammed still has the half payment for the camels and has not distributed the money to any of the owners. The arguments, the patient mediating, the differing factions, and the volume of advice pitches around the room continually.

I recognize half a dozen faces from Wadi Rumm - they have travelled all this way to bring Mohammed to justice and collect their share of the money. The state of the two sick camels is a further problem, and they argue that Mohammed is a bad handler, pushing his animals too far, too fast. They are very tribal proceedings, and, as at Rumm, James and I are forgotten. I now wish that I had bought the camels and not hired them - at least then I would be able to push them as hard as I wanted in order to achieve our aim.

Once more, Mohammed is single-handedly and doggedly fighting for what he wants. He delivers his case with such conviction and innocence that I am not sure it is he who is wrong. His is the handsomest face in the crowd and he exudes a dignity and grace among these rougher looking Bedouin. Even if he is an old rogue, I have a soft spot for him. Provided he gets us to journey's end on time I do not care where the money goes.

It is nearly 11 pm and the heat has gone out of the argument. Mohammed, having looked bored for the past half hour, stands up and motions us to go. I decide to remain and talk the problem through with the police officer who has a limited command of English - after the last three hours I am more confused than ever, but do not wish to discuss my queries with a group which ranges from a sheik to an off-duty policeman and a half-blind, half-deaf old man from Jafr. Mohammed looks cross as though he feels betrayed. He leaves on his own.

The gathering slowly disperses through the office door that opens onto the sandy courtyard of the fort. Only Hamad remains, humble and subservient in his manner, obviously feeling bad about his intention to speak ill of Mohammed behind his back. He tells us that Mohammed is a bad man, that he does not understand camels, that he cannot travel in a straight line but wanders wasteful miles across the desert, and, finally, that he is not happy to be paid off at this stage and entrust all six camels to Mohammed's care. After he leaves James and I, somewhat guiltily, eat bread and goat's cheese brought to us. We consider waking Chris and Mark to share it but lack the energy to actually do so - our bones ache with weariness... 'Tomorrow everything will be good, in shaa Allah,' says the officer. 'In shaa Allah.'

20 February

We sit in the school building at El Jafr facing the grandson of Auda Abu Tayi. Unfortunately his father Mohammed, who fought with Lawrence and Auda as a boy, is in Amman seeing his doctor. He did not ride by camel but chose his Mercedes instead - today the two are interchangeable. Although he is not the man we came to Jafr to seek, he is nonetheless of the same blood and his resemblance to the picture of Auda is marked. The circumstances and the setting are completely contrary to my expectations of this eagerly awaited scene. The meeting place is not a large Bedouin tent, piled deep with silks and rugs, brass coffee pots over the centre hearth, with the faces of desert warriors lit by the dancing firelight. Instead it is a schoolroom with wooden chairs on a cement floor, dirty walls with metal framed windows and military school teachers in uniform.

I am enchanted by his noble features. His face is the most beautiful of all the Bedouin we have seen, a reincarnation of the man so deeply revered by Lawrence. But when we speak of our venture and its connection with the history of his country, he shows complete indifference. The mention of 'El Aurens' and Auda produces no trace of recognition in his handsome face. His attitude seems to say that the past is dead and that the meaning of today is all that matters. He does not address us directly, but neither does he look straight at the other Bedu. It is not so much condescension as complete detachment. Apart from his beard - the mark of a man who has done a pilgrimage to Mecca - his finest features are his eyes. Somehow they have an amazing power that one associates with a natural leader. He has an electric effect on the other Jordanians, who proudly re-emphasise his connection with Abu Tayi when he leaves the room. As he goes I am aware of

Auda Abu Tayi whose grandson we met in the school building at El Jafr. Lawrence devoted several pages to a description of Auda in Seven Pillars of Wisdom, *testimony to the impression the Howeitat leader made on him.*

'*His face was magnificent in its lines and hollows. On it was written how truly the death in battle of Annad his favourite son, cast sorrow over all his life when it ended his dream of handing on to future generations the greatness of the name of Abu Tayi...His forehead was low and broad, his nose very high and sharp, powerfully hooked: his mouth rather large and mobile: his beard and moustaches had been trimmed*

to a point in Howeitat style, with the lower jaw shaven underneath.

'*He saw life as a saga. All the events in it were significant: all personages in contact with him heroic. His mind was stored with poems of old raids and epic tales of fights, and he overflowed with them on the nearest listener. If he lacked listeners, he would very likely sing them to himself in his tremendous voice, deep and resonant and loud... He spoke of himself in the third person, and was so sure of his fame that he loved to shout out stories against himself...*' Seven Pillars of Wisdom the extraordinary presence of the man and I regret not having photographed him or spoken directly of Lawrence and the Abu Tayi in the Arab Revolt.

The meeting was characteristic of a day when events seemed to take several turns, each one leaving me in doubt about the possibility of leaving for Bayir the next day with a full complement of camels, or even of the expedition continuing in its present form.

At first light the camel owners from Wadi Rumm had gathered around us where we slept on the ground outside the fort. They had argued and haggled over several conflicting solutions to a problem I could hardly see: all five camels were to return to Rumm; Mohammed was no good at navigation and was a bad man keeping all the money; if we continue, a Toyota pick-up must follow bringing fodder for the camels to ease their burden; we were to stay at Jafr two days and rest; and, finally, the camels were too tired to go on. And so it continued, over and over again, until I nearly screamed for some order in it all.

I had remained huddled in my sleeping bag somewhat perplexed by the verbal assault. Visibility was down to 50 metres from the sand borne by a lashing wind. Hungry and cold, feeling like a leper on the outskirts of a village, I decided that the expedition had reach a crossroads. A further round of talks at the police fort produced nothing. Khader merely informed us we could not leave until the money problem had been satisfactorily solved. He would decide when. I know now it was his patrol that visited us last night.

Crouched six to eight in the back of the Toyota pick-ups we were driven with great gusto through Jafr to the local school. The headmaster spoke excellent English and showed infinite patience in dealing with this problem that had been thrust upon him. The council of war - as James described it - met for the third time. Suddenly, just when it appeared that the same old arguments would once again lead us nowhere, a solution was found. The hatchets were buried and the men of Rumm left, smiling with assurances of Hashan's prowess as a camel, and wishing us as much success as Allah could possibly allow. We remained utterly bemused. The only agreement was that Hamad remained with the expedition on the same pay as Mohammed and that Mohammed would bring two fresh camels from Rumm.

Somehow honour had been satisfied. Hamad thanked me in the humblest way imaginable and I was ashamed though touched by his display of servility.

The major highlight of the negotiations was Mohammed's agreement that Abdulla should leave the expedition. He would return with his father. I was surprised to discover my intense loathing of the boy, next to the fondness I was beginning to feel for Mohammed and Hamad. I knew that we would be on a better footing as soon as the six of us left Jafr with the new camels.

Fresh provisions were purchased from the temporary looking

buildings that serve as shops. A baker was found among the sprawl of Bedu tents, brick houses, tin shacks and crumbling mud walls, which is the village of Jafr. The two weakest camels were skilfully settled into the back of the pick-ups, and looking a weird hybrid half-camel and half-Toyota, they were driven at break neck speed towards Wadi Rumm.

It was at that moment that my tenderly nurtured expectations about life in the desert were finally dissipated - for the modern Bedouin there is no adventure more than hours away. The camels couched in the pick-ups seemed to symbolise their changing life. Their expressions almost said 'Why bother with me now? My four legs take seven days, your wheels take but a few hours.'

As I watched them depart, the camels facing rear through a cloud of exhaust fumes and choking dust, I wondered why indeed.

Mohammed told me once why the camel always looked so smug and content. It was because Allah has a hundred names, of which the Arab knows ninety-nine. Only the camel knows the hundredth.

'Their birth set them in crowded places. An unintelligible passionate yearning drove them out into the desert.' Seven Pillars of Wisdom

Chapter Five

21 February

We awoke to a cloudy sky and a bitterly cold wind. After watering the camels at the police fort we moved off at 8.30 am. All day long we walked the camels; it was too cold to ride. Heads bent against a strong north-westerly wind we plodded across the endless Jafr mudflat heading north-east. We halted at 11.30 am and formed a wind-break with bags of camel fodder. With a small fire going and hot, sweet tea, we sat, apathetic, not wishing to leave the little warmth and rest to continue the journey.

Thankfully we were travelling over shingle rather than sand and so the wind was unaccompanied by dust.

By nightfall we have covered over 20 miles and are all extremely tired. We make a fire near some camel thorn in the middle of the plain, there being no other suitable shelter.

I zip up the sleeping bag tightly around me, but to no avail. In spite of the thobe, a thick sweater, and the head-cloth wrapped over my head, I can still feel the cold of the desert night. In vain I try to create a warm pocket of air which might stop me shivering. My eyes ache with tiredness yet I cannot sleep. In the darkness I make out the two camels resting where they were couched and hobbled earlier. I can only wonder at their resilience under such harsh conditions - the heavy loads they carry by day over many miles, the fact that they are left tied in the same position throughout the long night hours. I can hear them burping and their stomachs rumbling deeply as they regurgitate their last meal of grain.

Despite the discomfort of the day's travel I am elated that the expedition is safely en route to Bayir. The incident at Jafr with the camel owners had threatened our venture, and on reflection I know we have passed through a major crisis. If the problem with the payment of the camels had remained unsettled I could see all the mounts returning to Rumm in the owners' Toyota pick-ups. Now with two fresh camels, and Abdulla out of the way, I feel more in control of our goal.

Lying on my front and clutching a small torch between my teeth I flick through my diary. I estimate that between Wadi Rumm and El Jafra we covered 135 miles. Our present route is through Bayir to Azraq in the north of Jordan which will be a further 180 miles. It will be a similar journey, only in reverse, to the one that Lawrence took in November 1917 when he left Azraq for Aqaba. Now we are more accustomed to the desert and the Bedouin, I do not anticipate many problems in reaching Azraq

Re-packing near Bayir.

within a week - provided, God willing, the camels do not become sick.

To date the problem - for me at least - has not been the physical exertion of living in the desert so much as the mental strain of coping with the Bedouin. I remember that this was one of Wilfred Thesiger's observations in *Arabian Sands*. In fact I am surprised how quickly we have adjusted to the rigours of the journey - the meagre food each day, the long hours of travel, and the extreme variations in temperature. The only sign of illness has been my recent attack of diarrohea, and I hope this is not an ominous sign - should any of us suffer from dysentery it will be a different story.

'Our route through Bayir to Azraq will be a similar journey, only in reverse, to the one that Lawrence took in November 1917 when he left Azraq for Aqaba...I am fascinated by his account. Lawrence covered the journey in approximately twelve hours...the same arduous route takes us nearly two and a half days.'

22 February

We sit around a good-sized fire in the Wadi Bayir about 8 miles from Bayir itself. The flames leap high against another beautiful Arabian night sky. To the east there rises a pencil-thin line of the moon with the brilliant Venus near it. To any traveller the setting would seem perfect. To the reader the scene might conjure up the classic and clichéd pictures that belong to romantic desert stories. I finish writing my diary; it is surprising how much mental

'Hamad grew in personality as the expedition went on, he would start challenging a lot more.'

Mohammed at Wadi ash Shaumare.

'Mohammed was Mohammed the whole time.'

'The Bedouin could not look for God within him: he was too sure that he was within God. He could not conceive anything which was or was not God, Who alone was great... Arabs felt no incongruity in bringing God into the weakness and appetites of their least creditable causes...' Seven Pillars of Wisdom

discipline is required to do this simple thing, but it would be easier to gaze into the warm flickering flames, drink tea, and make idle conversation.

Another hard day, particularly as the ground was flint boulders all the way, and again a very cold wind despite a cloudless sky. We have laughed a lot this evening at Hamad's expense concerning the goat's cheese that we bought in Jafr. Mohammed claimed it made Hamad a little mad and homosexual. In fact the cheese was extremely salty, but Hamad rose to the bait and threw it away. Now we worry in case the camels eat it. I am surprised how much communication has developed with the Bedouin, despite the absence of a common language.

My camel Hashan is showing signs of playing up. Today he has been a particular nuisance, sitting down when he felt like it, and on one occasion I accidentally let the rein go and he bolted off across the desert. I watched with interest how the Bedouin coaxed him back. Apparently it was caused by tiredness, and the overall endurance of a camel is something I have failed to measure in planning the venture.

We stopped in the Wadi ash Shaumare at 11.00 am Here was the first grass that I have seen in the desert, and it seemed completely out of place. It was indeed a tranquil and lush setting and we were reluctant to move on. Hamad found a shrub whose leaves contain salt; there were a number of birds in the wadi, too, particularly black and white Wheatears, the size of a thrush. Also we put up a rabbit in the afternoon that raced terrified across the desert.

The camels maintained a fair pace and we covered about 22 miles. However I had hoped to reach Bayir by dusk, and we might have done had we not had to by-pass a fairly formidable jebel range that suddenly appeared out of an otherwise featureless plain.

23 February

Mohammed is always the first to rise and light a fire to boil the water. He squats there as I walk among the others to rouse them. The routine is automatic after ten days, little is said and each man attends to his needs and his camel without instructions. The early morning sky is deep blue, and with no wind there is promise of a fine day. A whisper of white frost colours the rocks in the wadi. Our bivvy bags are stiff as boards and the water containers have frozen in the night - even the hair of the camels is overlaid with the morning silver.

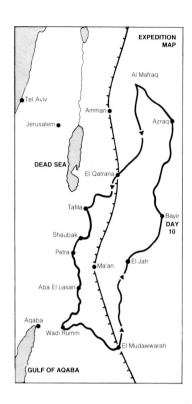

On the horizon to the East I detect the faint outline of a desert fort overlooking the wadi. Mohammed confirms it to be Bayir. With keen optimism at the sight of the next objective, we load the camels and lead them down the rocky incline. Small boulders, loose under foot, make the going hard, and walking in sandals increases the soreness of my feet. The camels tread tentatively and we make for the wadi bottom where the ground is not so rough.

Mohammed sings and Hamad walks to the rear, repeating each line. The echoing chant fills the dawn air. It is a happy song, refreshing in its simplicity and sincere delivery. I wish I understood its theme; it is their first open expression of content-ment, a moment to be savoured.

After travelling for three and a half hours our caravan reaches the end of the wadi. In front a steep slope rises in natural defence towards the fort hidden by the dead ground above. We ascend slowly, the camels taking large leaps forward when they lose their footing on the rough ground. I stop to enjoy the panorama which our high vantage point affords, admiring the rich yellow and brown colours of the desert to the west.

I notice below, at the end of the other fork in the wadi, an irregular gathering of stone piles and what appear to be old wells. They must be the ones Lawrence described that were dynamited by the Turks in April 1917 to prevent their use by his forces. The mounds would be the graves he mentioned where Auda's favourite son lies buried. One can almost imagine the scene of the Arab army camped there. The scene is perfectly preserved as Lawrence saw it - the only such identifiable example since the immovable rocks of Rumm

Cresting the hill we near the high walls of the fort; its smooth lines project directly from the bare rock and in style it seems more akin to a small Crusader castle. The rifle slits and ramparts dominate our line of approach - we might be feudal serfs approaching the castle of a ruling lord.

We couch and unload the camels a short distance from the front gate tower. A sentry stands guard, smartly dressed in long khaki overcoat, brass buttons, red leather cross-straps with glint-ing cartridges and rifle in hand. A half square of painted white stones demarcates a parade area around the main entrance - even

The author and Mohammed at Wadi ash Shaumare.

'Among the Arabs there were no distinctions, traditional or natural, except the unconscious power given a famous sheikh by virtue of his accomplishment; and they taught me that no man could be their leader except he ate the rank's food, wore their clothes, lived level with them, and yet appeared better in himself.' Seven Pillars of Wisdom

in the desert it imposes a military order. A smiling gathering of Desert Police leads us to rugs laid in our honour by the walls. We relax in the warm sun, content in achieving another goal, eagerly anticipating their hospitality, and looking forward to the visit by the Defence Attaché. At El Jafr I had managed to contact the Embassy and assure them of our continuing existence and safety. Colonel David Whitten intended driving across the desert to meet at Bayir by midday - the estimated time of our arrival.

It is now 10 pm. We welcome the rest after the continual daily mileage required to achieve our aim of completing 1,000 miles.

Over nine hours each day are spent either walking or riding, and although hardened by the rigour we are worn by the frugal existence.

In spite of there being normal cooking facilities in the fort, we sit around a fire on which the inevitable pots of coffee and tea are kept warm. There is no shade and soon we become very warm where we sit directly facing the sun. By comparison the soldiers crowd around the fire, and I become aware of how important this feature is in their tribal way of life. Initially there is a buzz of animated conversation caused by our arrival, and the soldiers are very curious of the Englishmen who dress as Arabs and travel by camel.

I become tired of the attention, and for want of privacy I turn instead to *Seven Pillars of Wisdom*. I begin to read of Lawrence's times at Bayir and of the long journey by camel from Azraq to Aqaba. The strength of his writing is refreshing especially since it distracts me from the present. The concentration required to take in the meaning and implications of each sentence stimulates my mind after the limited vocabulary needed during the day.

Immediately, I am fascinated by his account of the journey between Bayir and Jafr on 24/25 November, 1917. He writes of having a 'heavy bout of fever on me', yet accompanied by one Arab he succeeded in covering overnight our same journey of 55 miles, albeit in the other direction. Lawrence records how 'we passed Bair long after dark, when only its latest tent-fires still shone', and 'in the forenoon we reached Auda's camp'. From his approximate timings I try to work out an estimate for ourselves: assuming 'long after dark' meant around 10.00 pm, and 'forenoon' meant 10.00 am, Lawrence covered the journey in approximately twelve hours, of which one hour may be deducted for the watering of the camels and another half hour for easing them afterwards. I make a few calculations and realise he must have covered at least 4 to 5 miles every hour to have accomplished the journey, the majority of it in darkness. The same arduous route had taken us twenty hours travelling by daylight, and, all told, nearly two and a half days.

Remembering the appalling terrain we covered, particularly the last 10 to 15 miles through the wadis Shaumari and Bayir, I read again Lawrence's account and check my deductions. To cover 4 to 5 miles in an hour cannot be achieved at the normal walking speed of a camel - certainly in our experience. Furthermore, to maintain that speed over rough country in the pitch dark of a November's night, and with a heavy bout of fever, seems all the more remarkable. If Lawrence's account is accurate (and my calculations correct) it was a tremendous feat - if not impossible. Even if he had been going at a more sedate pace of 3 miles an hour, it still would have taken him eighteen hours solid riding.

I do not relish these doubts. Even though we are the first expedition to retrace some of his journeys by camel, and under similar conditions, it was never our intention to 'test' his achievements. Yet even accounting for his acknowledged prowess as a rider, the fine condition of his mount, (which in any case he had not changed since Azraq), and the urgency of his ride, there is an obvious discrepancy between our journeys. At the same time, I realise the danger of taking too literal a view of his account - many people more qualified than me have suggested a number of embellishments and exaggerations in *Seven Pillars of Wisdom*. I ask Mohammed and the assembled audience of Arabs whether it would be possible to complete the journey in one day with a good camel. He does not think so. I tell him of Lawrence's claim and he laughs, asking me whether he did it by car. Certainly I know that with our animals we could not possibly have covered the distance any faster - it was bad enough by day and I would not have wished to have ridden it by night.

Once more Mohammed asks to see my blue book. Proudly he shows the soldiers the pictures of Lawrence and Auda. They recognise their own Howeitat warrior immediately, and as each man speaks of Auda the others nod in sincere agreement.

So we sit outside the fort on rugs and cushions, basking contented in the sun and sharing a little of their conversation. With our soiled clothes, beards and growing confidence with the language and etiquette of the Bedouin, I feel we have blended in at last. These soldiers are happy and talkative, they do not deride our appearance or intentions, rather they admire our journey. And of Lawrence? Well, they reply, he is known as a great Englishman but Glubb Pasha is the father of their army.

'Do we know Glubb?' the short and jovial officer in command of the fort asks.

'Yes,' I reply. 'He has written to me, and before leaving England I spoke with him.'

They beam with delight and awe. Several excited questions are asked and then the stories of Glubb Pasha abound - how he built their fort, raised their army and would deliberately put lice on himself before visiting so that he could say he was the same as them.

They are talking of thirty years ago. Lieutenant-General Sir John Bagot Glubb, KCB, CMG, DSO, OBE, MC had commanded the Arab Legion from 1939 to 1956, although his involvement as a seconded officer in the service of the Jordanian Government had begun in 1930. Under him the Jordanian army grew and the security of the ill-defined borders with neighbouring countries was improved. The Arab Legion had seconded British officers and was modelled firmly on British Army lines, the characteristics of which are retained today. Glubb established a chain of Desert Police forts at intervals in the desert hinterland towards Arabia. They were manned by soldiers of the Legion with a brief to stamp out intertribal rivalry and camel raiding, and bring the tribes of Jordan to a more cohesive, new state. For centuries they had been nomads living according to their own tribal customs.

The work of this one Englishman, and General Peake before him, did much to eradicate the anti-British feeling following the displacement of the Palestinians by the state of Israel.

Lieutenant-General Sir John Bagot Glubb *who commanded the Arab Legion from 1939 to 1956.*

'The Bedouin are completely unpolitical. Mohammed would cross the border to Israel as if the desert is theirs and the political demarcations by statesmen have no meaning.
Government policy in Jordan is to bring the Bedu into towns, establish a fixed population... Before Jordan there were lots of warring tribes, camel stealing. Sir John Glubb in the late '30s brought in a backbone of security with the Arab Legion.'

At the forts of Rumm and El Jafr the sincerity of the affectionate memories of Glubb Pasha had been the same.

'Reckon we should've been following him then instead of Lawrence,' remarks Mark in his down-to-earth manner.

We doze gently in the sun after a fine meal served on a variety of dishes, right where we sit. I study the long route north to Azraq - there are no settlements or wells marked on the map, and Mohammed estimates four to five days for the journey. It is the very limit of our water-carrying capability, and already two small containers leak so badly as to be useless. The soldiers bring us a spare one along with more salt, tea and sugar. I ask Mohammed about the food but he says they have none to spare at the fort, or more likely he will not ask them for some reason known to himself alone. Despite the two fresh camels, their overall performance and speed is not remarkable by the standards I had been led to expect before leaving England. Our timings are critical and it remains a constant worry to follow our schedule.

I still feel we are not yet fully prepared for the rigours of the journey to Azraq. Also I had hoped to purchase more provisions at Bayir, thinking there was a Bedu village here. In fact the fort is the only building, standing solitary and imposing on the high ground - the sweeping panorama of desert, undulating low hills and wadis, extends to the horizon and only the rusted wreck of an old army lorry hints at any encroachment.

From the advantage of the high ground I spot a white landrover far off. There are no roads and I watch the dust cloud behind the vehicle increase as it covers the undulating terrain. Eventually it arrives and stops by the sentry box, a ramshackle wooden affair painted with the national colours of Jordan. I walk to greet David Whitten and Rosemary and only when I am close does he recognise us. They did not think the fort was actually Bayir, or that the couched camels, Bedouins and soldiers dozing in the sun had anything British about them. After a mere ten days' exposure to the sun, they notice a profound change in our appearance. It is as though we have gone native, an impression they suggest that is not entirely due to our dress. By comparison they look very pale and almost out of place amid it all.

'The first white man or woman we've seen in ten days,' quips Chris.

With the need to push on towards Azraq we repay their generosity poorly when we load the camels after one hour. There had been so many colourful experiences to describe, but somehow our conversation is awkward. Although our time in the desert has been short it has given us a new identity. We have tried to shed our Western prejudices and beliefs, to assume our new role, yet at the same time we retain characteristics of our upbringing.

I feel I am trying to live in two different worlds at the same time - one moment accepting a cold beer from David and the next realising how alcohol offends the Bedouin, and that I cannot be

'We treasure our insular, isolated life in the desert... We have tried to shed our Western prejudices and beliefs, to assume our new role, yet at the same time we retain characteristics of our upbringing...'

one with them if I accept such Western luxuries so readily. I know we cannot shake off who we are and forget about the outside world in one month (although this is what I want to do).

We pose for photographs, some standing and others mounted on our camels. It is frustrating trying to keep the camels still and in line. James and I stretch the regimental flag between us and our mounts do everything possible to prevent it from unfurling properly.

We ride north, gently swaying in motion together. I turn to wave as we sever our links with our friends once more (and gladly so). Despite the kindness of people, we treasure our insular, isolated life in the desert. Frequent contacts threaten to erode it to the point where James even objects if an old vehicle track is seen in the sand. Again I know we must be realistic and accept it. But I am trying to find something in this desert...only I am not sure what it is.

'Hashan ques?' asks Hamad as he rides beside me.

'Awah Ham, Hashan ques al Hamdu Lilla.'

He smiles broadly and hands over some dirty sunflower seeds. Our hands just reach each other's as we move with the rhythm of our mounts. He then begins to sing, and repeats the chant of the morning. Mohammed responds and this gentle lullaby caresses us and reminds us of the Bedouin charm.

I look back to Bayir one last time and note we are passing a short distance from the historic Chassarid wells. Lawrence had spent his thirtieth birthday encamped there, an occasion 'to satisfy my sense of sincerity, I began to dissect my beliefs and motives...Indeed, the truth was I did not like the "myself" I could see and hear.'

Chapter Six

24 February

The lice have arrived, creating a new topic of conversation that eclipses all other concerns. Chris and James seem relatively immune for the moment, but Mark and I itch, scratch and curse vigorously hunting the vermin, using riding sticks to reach inaccessible parts of our backs.

We walk for the first two hours of the morning, our route going across wadis and low hills, sapping much of our precious energy. Hashan behaves awkwardly and on several occasions crashes to the ground as if to indicate he will go no further. The third time is too much. I glare at him, tug hard on the rein, and raise my stick in anger - it is only an urgent shout from Hamad that stops me delivering the threatened blow. Hashan curls his lips back and spits and bellows in defiance. My early affection for the animal is fading fast. Handing over the rein of his camel, Hamad begins to unload the water containers, sacks and saddle bags from Hashan. I stare up at his mount, envious of its more placid nature. Two large brown eyes return my stare dismissively, the animal's rubbery jaw constantly moving sideways, up and down, while he chews a clump of thorn bush.

Hamad finishes re-saddling Hashan. Mohammed watches, squatting to rest on his heels right up to the last moment, only rising once we move again.

We reach a small wadi covered in delicate white and purple wild flowers. Fragile, they hide among thorn clusters and behind small boulders, yet still cannot escape the feverish search of hungry camels, who devour this luxurious grazing like desert hoovers. I take a photograph as everyone collects handfuls of greenery. Mohammed gathers his robes about him and fills the fold with flowers, walking on ahead offering the occasional sprig to his eager camel.

It seems sacrilege to pick the flowers, whose survival amid this desolate and barren emptiness is surely a miracle of nature, but the opportunity to tease the animals is not passed over: Chris's mount, which is normally the slowest, strains forward to reach the tantalising morsels in his outstretched hand and literally doubles his pace.

Once again Mohammed and I disagree over the route. Concerned for the health of the camels and the general shortage of food and water, I want to go north - the most direct route to Azraq. But since Bayir Mohammed has led us north-west.

Presently Mohammed points to three prominent and unusually shaped mountains which rise out of the black flint desert in the distance. 'Thlaithukhwat,' he says while riding towards what must have been landmarks for generations of traders with their camel trains.

Shortly after midday we pass to their left, stopping for a rest to graze the camels on the far side. I search through *Seven Pillars of Wisdom* to find Mohammed yet again correct, for travelling between Bayir and Azraq on 1 November, 1917, Lawrence wrote: 'Next day we passed to the left of the Thlaithukhwat, the "Three Sisters" whose clean white peaks were landmarks on their lofty watershed for a day's journey about; and went down the soft rolling slopes beyond them.'

'Yallah, yallah! Rope!' Mohammed shouts when we are ready to leave. With my left foot firm along the rein forcing Hashan's head down and the rope end in my hand as I face rear, I tentatively ease my right leg over the saddle. However, a slight downwards pressure, caused by my calf inadvertently touching the saddle, makes Hashan leap suddenly to his feet and bolt forward in one move. Four feet above the ground, and accelerating to a fast gallop, I cling desperately to the front pommel with both hands. My right leg points to the sky with my left bent double to avoid the rough surface. Hashan races with his head barely inches above the ground. My kaffiyah flies off and with one supreme effort I haul myself into the bouncing saddle, the front pommel crushing into the soft centre of my body each time it comes up as I go down. After a few hundred metres Hashan halts, looks at me, then quietly lowers his head to nibble the top of a thorn bush. Chris later describes it as Charles's 'Dash with Hash', but I use stronger language at the time.

At least 30 miles are covered by dusk, and we are weary from the constant cross-wadiing in our attempt to steer straight for Azraq. James begins the nightly star fix while we sit around the bright fire, its flames leaping higher and sharper than normal. It is the warmest night of the expedition and we perspire freely. I produce the unopened medicinal bottle of whisky, and it is greeted with cries of 'Hubbly, Hubbly Bubbly!' by our Bedouin.

Mohammed refuses to allow it to be drunk in his presence, pointing a finger to his head and saying, 'Hubbly Bubbly not good.' Despite his humour I understand their religion and put aside the offending article. Instead, as though sensing our need for light relief, he turns the conversation to sex. It is the first time the Bedu have mentioned it, and I am surprised by the sudden familiarity. The firelight covers his face in mischievous lines, his teeth shine brilliant white and tears roll down his face in unrestrained laughter, until eventually he finds breath to speak his thoughts.

'Ham...Ham,' he squeals slapping Hamad on the back, 'He has two wives but very small...' and he demonstrates before falling over onto the grain sacks in an uncontrollable fit. 'Mohammed, he and camel same same!' retorts Hamad not to be outdone. We laugh.

Changing his theme, Mohammed is back on stage: 'Ames,' he chuckles pointing to the shadowy figure against the stars, his head close to the theodolite, 'Ames...big foot...bom...bom... bom...' With his hands he imitates two feet going across the desert.

He repeats the performance, beside himself with laughter.

It is true, James wears his black army boots continually despite the heat, and his feet *are* enormous. It is this and his preference for walking more often than the rest of us, which have occasioned the remark. The Bedu are fascinated by the tall figure of 'Ames', head bent and deep in thought, arms behind his back holding the rein, his two huge boots pounding across the sand from beneath his robes.

We are happy that an affinity appears to be developing in spite of our stark differences. Away from the pressures of day-to-day life in the West we gradually rediscover the pleasures of communicating: simple things normally forgotten assume great importance; a joke can be made to last for many days, each time binding us together in its telling and in reliving shared experiences.

James' boots which he insisted on wearing. Lawrence's men were more concerned with hats -

'*Our persistence in the hat (due to a misunderstanding of the ways of heat-stroke) had led the East to see significance in it, and after long thought their wisest brains concluded that Christians wore the hideous thing that its broad brim might interpose between their weak eyes and the uncongenial sight of God... The British thought this prejudice reprehensible (quite unlike our hatred of a head-cloth) one to be corrected at any price. If the people would not have us hatted, they should not have us any way.*'
Seven Pillars of Wisdom

25 February

My diary reads: 'I lay awake last night, smoking and thinking. It was very warm with a quarter moon. At times the sky was alive with shooting stars. I thought of my life and the future. The pain of D and the decision over T and the army, and whether I am correct.

'I had a strange dream. I was waiting to walk a plank or log between two land masses. Beneath, there lay a vast, sea of unknown. Several people had successfully crossed it before me. I stepped on with confidence but as I reached the middle I lost my balance and only just managed to regain it. As I was about to fall I glanced down and there, below, among the multitude of faces, I could make out only one. He was a friend of mine who had committed suicide. He smiled at me and slowly beckoned with his outstretched arm. The picture was so vivid, it was clearly him. I continued to walk, only to find my right foot slipping - I toppled, but again managed to stay on. Reaching the end I turned to wave. He smiled, beckoned once more, and then I lost my balance, pitching over backwards into the unknown.

'We stopped early this evening because Mohammed did a complete sit-down on us. All day we have battled along through hills and wadis against a bitterly cold and strong wind. It was such that I can only compare it to the wind of the Welsh mountains in winter. It also rained hard. A thoroughly miserable and dispiriting day.

'The camels shivered badly in the cold, and we had to stop at midday to light a fire to dry ourselves off. We covered only about 15 miles. At one stage the wind tore the map from my hands, and I had to race 600 yards in anxious pursuit. It caught on a thorn bush, so all was not lost.

26 February

No water remains. We are too cold to care and too bruised by the wind to think. The glamour of the desert is gone. The laughter of the past is replaced by complaints and swearing. Clouds scud above us, dark and grey. We look no further than a foot ahead, bowed over to balance the invisible force that chills our bodies. It rains intermittently.

Mohammed's camel limps badly. Hamad walks miserably beside me, his khaki coat concealing all but two shuffling feet below his naked ankles. His plimsolls are as torn and useless as the old trekking shoes from Nepal that I wear. Hamad moans loudly and wraps his coat still more closely about him. At the rear, Chris drags his camel, frequently having to urge it on with his stick. The animals are in a wretched state and suffer the cold badly. Rivulets of water run down their dark brown fur, and they shiver uncontrollably, each stiff-legged step an enormous effort.

Suddenly, out of nowhere, a huge, dark yellow earth-mover, almost 10 foot high, with ugly, black tyres, roars past. The driver, dry and warm in his cab, sounds the horn loudly, scattering the animals.

'Where's the Lawrence of Arabia music now?' shouts Mark in my ear. Where indeed. A long scar cutting to the left is the new road being built from Ma'an to Azraq. The experience makes me feel ridiculous, out-of-time, redundant in the desert of today.

Bitterly we claw our way across the grey landscape buffeted on all sides by the force of the wind. Now I appreciate first-hand the harsh misery of Lawrence's more difficult journeys, though for us, at least, there is no disease, no heat exhaustion to withstand.

The Roman castle at Azraq became Lawrence's headquarters in the winter of 1917. Set amid a lava field, and surrounded by palm trees and the Roman fish ponds, it was a place for which Lawrence had great affection. It inspired his writing and, at the time, eased his tortured soul.

By November of that year Lawrence had been actively engaged in the Revolt for just over twelve months. The political and military campaigning had been hard. He was privy to the information of the secret Sykes-Picot agreement between the British and the French - an agreement which divided the post-war Middle East of the defeated Ottoman Empire into the imperial interests of those countries. Far from unifying the Arabs and giving them independence, as Lawrence promised in his role as mediator between Emir Feisal and the British, it replaced one overlord with another. He resented the betrayal. In August 1918 he wrote of honour: 'had I not lost that a year ago when I assured the Arabs that England kept her plighted word?' and 'I exploited their highest ideals and made their love of freedom one more tool to help England win.'

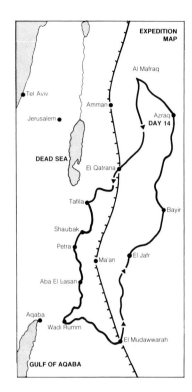

The castle at Azraq became the forward base for Lawrence and the Arab army. Their own major supply base at Aqaba - captured in June 1917 (an action for which Lawrence was recommended the Victoria Cross) had moved inland to shorten the lines of communication. The area in between, however, had not been totally subjugated by Turkish forces who still relied upon the strategic Hejaz railway. It was a very fluid and irregular war.

On 4 November, 1917, Lawrence arrived at Azraq having ridden from Bayir on the night of 31 October. Later he wrote, 'We hurried up the stoney ridge in high excitement, talking of the wars and songs and passions of the early shepherd kings, with names like music, who had loved this place; and of the Roman legionaries who languished here as a garrison in yet earlier times. The blue fort on its rock above the rustling palms, with the fresh meadows and shining springs of water, broke on our sight. Of Azraq, as of Rumm, one said "Numen inest." Both were magically haunted: but whereas Rumm was vast and echoing and God-like, Azraq's unfathomable silence was steeped in a knowledge of wandering poets, champions, lost kingdoms, all the crime and chivalry and dead magnificence of Hira and Ghassan. Each stone or blade of it was radiant with half memory of the luminous silky Eden, which had passed so long ago.'

One journey from Azraq ended in an experience at Deraa which became the crux of *Seven Pillars of Wisdom*. In late November 1917 he set off on a reconnaisance to study the feasibility of cutting the Hejaz railway there - a successful raid would not only have considerable military advantages but would demoralise the Turkish garrison. According to his own account he was captured by the Turks, beaten up, whipped, and then buggered by the Bey of Deraa. The account has been questioned by subsequent authors. However, there can be little doubt that a major and traumatic event occurred.

Lawrence escaped and managed to return to Azraq. Two days later he left by camel for Aqaba riding via Bayir and El Jafr.

'There are many things I could say of the Deraa incident,' Tom Beaumont said to me when I had visited him before the expedition departed. 'But I would never tell a soul. My mouth has remained closed for nearly sixty years and it will stay that way... Sufficient to say that when we picked him up in the desert near Azraq and brought him back, his clothes were bloodied and torn.'

Arriving at the Crusader Castle at Azraq.

'We dreamed ourselves into the spirit of the place; sieges and fasting, raids, murders, love-singing in the night.'
Seven Pillars of Wisdom

27 February

We arrive at Azraq castle and make our way quietly in single file. It is long past sunset and an old man lights our passage by lantern. He holds it up to see his own way clearly over the worn step, through a huge door of basalt 1 foot thick, and under the gate tower towards the courtyard. A black ring of dragons' teeth, set against silhouettes of wavering palm trees, bare themselves open to the stars. It is eerily silent.

In the yellow light the shadows of the rocks shift, stretching away, distorting, concealing and finally throwing themselves into relief once more. The light guides us up the small flight of stone stairs from the sand below to a room above the gate-tower. The old man stands in the middle of the earth floor breathless after the walk. He holds the lantern just above his shoulder as we survey the room - walls of roughly hewn thick black basalt - a small room with three arrow slits to the world outside.

The castle is normally locked and deserted by night, but a chance meeting with the castle's custodian secured the privilege to visit Lawrence's room. And after the nature of our journey was explained, he bent gracefully to our insistence that we be allowed to sleep one night there. His father, he tells us, had fought with Lawrence.

It is the same room over the southern gate tower where Lawrence slept and worked in 1917. And it was to this room that he returned after Deraa.

We have forged another link. I look through an arrow slit. The nearby street lamps do not reveal the 'silky Eden' that Lawrence once described, but instead a road with traffic and occasional shack serving as a shop. A military convoy rumbles past heading south - a different war and a different place. Only inside have we trapped time.

We lay our sleeping bags on the soft earth floor. Only Hamad has stayed with the camels and camped among the tamarisk and palms nearby.

The old man leaves, and the castle is quiet except for the odd vehicle horn and the mosque summoning people to prayer. After the unexpected hardship of the journey from Bayir the peaceful confinement suits us well and we relish the contiguity with history. By the light of the lantern beside me I read extracts from *Seven Pillars*, about Lawrence's time at Azraq. The others lie in their sleeping bags and listen attentively.

'In the evening, when we had shut-to the gate, all guests would assemble, either in my room or in Ali's, and coffee and stories would go round until the last meal, and after it, until sleep came. On stormy nights we brought in brushwood and dung and lit a great fire in the middle of the floor. About it would be drawn the carpets and the saddle-sheepskins, and in its light we would tell over our own battles, or hear the visitor's traditions. The leaping flames chased our smoke-ruffled shadows strangely about the rough stone wall behind us, distorting them over the hollows and projections of its broken face...'

I stop to study the ground between Mark and I. Somewhere there. The others cast their eyes around the room observing the same shadowy effect. It is not difficult to imagine.

'When these stories came to a period,' continues Lawrence, 'our tight circle would shift over, uneasily, to the other knee or elbow; while coffee-cups went clinking round, and a servant fanned the blue reek of the fire towards the loophole with his cloak, making the ash swirl and sparkle with his draught... Past and Future flowed over us like an uneddying river. We dreamed ourselves into the spirit of the place; sieges and feasting, raids, murders, love-singing in the night.'

28 February.

We sit drinking the morning tea in the custodian's room and feel drugged by deep sleep, the result of this first night of shelter in two weeks. In the daylight the old man has extraordinarily blue eyes, apparently not uncommon in this area populated by Druze.

The walls carry several pictures of Lawrence in different guises. Altogether, it is a small shrine to Lawrence's memory: a sign in the castle's courtyard points to 'Lawrence's Room', but interestingly 'of Arabia' has been painted out; on a stone at the castle's entrance is carved 'Used by Lawrence'; in bold letters and underneath, almost as an afterthought, appears the history of this ancient place. Azraq is not so much known for the legacy of

the Roman occupation, or the Byzantines, as for its brief associa-
tion with a single man. It is as if this one Englishman has eclipsed
its two thousand-year history .

We return to Hamad and the camels and look back at the castle
through the palms; it is an ideal location for a day's reorganisa-
tion and rest - essential respite for both camels and men. I study
the map at length while the remainder wander Azraq's dirty
streets to purchase two weeks' provisions. The choice of route is
difficult. In the original plan the intention was to loop back
towards Bayir, head east to Wadi ash Sirhan, return to Azraq,
and pick up Lawrence's route again in Wadi Hesa near the Dead
Sea, finally retracing it to Aqaba.

But in fourteen days we have covered 315 miles - slow progress
compared with our original aim, and a far cry from Lawrence's
record, an average of 50 miles daily. I delete 300 miles and
change the route to head north-west to Mushrif and south by
Qatrana, Tafila to Aqaba. It is another disappointment, but we
cannot postpone our return to England on 18 March.

Later in the morning James and I loiter opposite the castle,
drinking tea with an old man who has a bazaar-like shop in a
shack made of tin and wood. We squat on the ground chatting
and smoking. The sun is out and we are refreshed by the opportunity to enjoy some time away from the routine of each day's
travel. A large coach draws up opposite. We watch with amusement as the tourists pour onto the street - an ocean of cameras;
the scene is not dissimilar to a Bateman cartoon.

All are French, and after two weeks in the desert with only
camels and Bedouin for company we eye the girls amongst them
appreciatively, disputing which one is the most attractive.

A French woman approaches. Standing 10 feet off and intent
on managing a complicated camera, she clicks away at the scene
of 'Bedouin', squatting in filth enjoying a midday yarn in Arab
fashion.

'Merci,' she says and turns to leave.

'You are most welcome,' answers James in his best Etonian
voice.

She does a double take. 'You speak English?' she asks in
surprise.

'We are English!'

She blushes beautifully, holding her hand in front of her face.
'But I thought you were blue-eyed Druze. We have heard so
much of them and I thought I had taken some good photographs.' We chuckle as she returns to the others and, pointing in
our direction, recounts the story.

The tourists disappear inside the castle for a quick tour, all but
a small Frenchman, who has separated himself from the main
party. He crosses the street with a large cine camera on his
shoulder. He appears to film everything. Suddenly his eyes light

on us and he advances with quick steps while adjusting the camera settings. Positioning himself in the middle of the road he is nearly flattened by an Arab driver. Then, taking the hint, he draws closer until he is barely 5 feet away. We perform with enthusiasm: James slurps his tea more loudly than ever before, after which he blows his nose into his head-cloth. Jabbering away in a mixture of Arabic amd Peter Sellers' French, we stroke our beards, spit on the ground between our legs and look suitably rogueish as if just returned from a tribal raid. The Frenchman loves it.

After filming for a few minutes he mutters to himself, looks around at the alien environment and scurries back to the safety of the coach. We laugh as we imagine the number of people that will now fall victim to our disguise, and at the sheer absurdity of travelling all the way to Jordan to film two British army officers instead of the real thing.

In the afternoon Mohammed becomes moody and unresponsive. On questioning him he becomes agitated and I fail to understand anything except that it is again about money. Hamad comes to the rescue, squatting beside us and arguing with Mohammed. The tension rises as they battle it out, gesticulating with their hands.

By chance I see the friend of the custodian approaching, a young Druze who speaks passable English. I ask him to help explain the problem.

'Mister, this man here, Mohammed, he says you must give him more money.'

'What for?'

'Mister Mohammed, he says you must pay the food for the camel.'

Furious, I ask him to tell Mohammed that it was agreed with Brigadier Shobaky in Aqaba that the money included fodder.

Mohammed remains adamant. For the first time I loathe him - one moment he is smiling and generous, the next deceitful and money-grabbing. It prompts a similar feeling to the one Lawrence had felt when he wrote, 'I was tired to death of these Arabs; petty incarnate Semites who attained heights and depths beyond our reach, though not beyond our sight. They realised our absolute in their unrestrained capacity for good and evil.'

'Mister, this man he says that you must eight hours only with camel in one day.'

'What?'

I stare at Mohammed itching to hit him. He only looks reproachful and his eyes are not vindictive. At a time when we are behind schedule, with 400 miles to cover in a fortnight, I find Mohammed is still trying to dictate the hours we can travel.

In a time of crisis James' cool sense of perspective is vital. I have never known him lose his temper, whereas I erupt in a flash. He normally effaces himself, allowing me to argue and dictate. I turn to him for support.

'Shobaky, you speak Shobaky,' says Mohammed. 'Mohammed finish.' He stands up and walks off towards the castle.

James suggests that it is because we are moving faster than Mohammed expected and as a result the camels are eating more grain. More grain means less money for Mohammed. It is a feasible explanation. Then it occurs to me that it may be related to an earlier incident.

In the morning Mohammed had returned to the camp site wearing a new leather and fur jacket he'd bought. He asked me to pay for his gloves but I declined. At the time he looked pretty upset about it all. Perhaps I should have paid as he is in my care, but at the end of the day we're giving him everything - even down to his cigarettes, about forty a day. I think of all the free advertising for our sponsors with those empty packets strewn across the desert.

I suggest getting some tea from the old boy at the shop and James agrees, saying he also needs to find some Mars bars.

We walk across the marsh grass and palm trees. Mohammed is seated talking to the shop keeper. I ignore him. He stands with dignity and draws two stools for us. He is smiling but I am sure he feels offended. However he pours the tea into the small glasses and offers a cigarette. I realise the incident is forgotten in his mind and it is only our Western way to harbour grudges. In the Arab world it is done and forgotten about - the same applied with the camel owners from Rumm, who one moment were ready to lynch him and the next minute they happily drove off together, back to their small Bedouin community.

I can't help feeling an affection for the man. Somehow he disarms my annoyance as easily as he provokes it. In the evening the six of us sit about the fire after the largest meal we have yet consumed. Preparations for a dawn departure are complete.

We gaze into the fire. The tension has gone, again we feel the bond of travelling. Chris asks Mark to play his mouth organ. He refuses and appears uncharacteristically quiet.

'You won't laugh at me if I tell you something will you?'

'Depends what it is.'

'No, serious like...you may think I'm a nutter. In fact I think I might be too after last night.'

'What do you mean?' I ask trying to encourage him.

'Well, last night, in the castle, I saw a ghost.' We crane forward and look at him, certain that he's having us on. Mark has never looked more serious.

'I don't know what time it was but I woke up suddenly. I looked up from my maggot* and there was this transparent wall in front of the real wall. You know where I was sleeping? Well, Mohammed was in the corner opposite and a bit to the left. The wall was on the other side , and I could tell it was transparent because Mohammed and the real wall were behind it.

* Army slang for sleeping bag.

It was a sort of yellowy grey colour and seemed to stop half way across the room. This end of it there was this figure, definitely the shape of a man. I couldn't distinguish any face but I vividly remember there was a wide shoulder strap slung across his body, seemed to me it was black, and around the hip hung a square box-shaped object. Didn't any of you wake up?'

We shake our heads.

'I thought I would've woken you, 'cause I talked to this ghost.'

We ask him what it said.

'Nothing, but I remember asking who he was and what did he want over and over again. I was terrified. You must think I'm crazy.'

We sit in silence. Mohammed adds more wood to the fire.

'Why didn't you tell us earlier?' I ask, adding that we could all have gone ghost hunting tonight.

'You'd not get me anywhere near that room again,' he replies. 'At one stage, I don't know after how long, it appeared to drift to my end of this transparent wall like a mist. It shimmered as it went. That was too much and I dived back under my maggot again. When I looked up later it was gone, and only Mohammed lay in the corner sleeping.'

'It certainly wasn't blinking Lawrence of Arabia,' jokes Chris.

'You don't believe me do you? I hadn't said anything before because I knew you'd think me crazy. I wasn't going to tell you at all,' Mark replies.

I explain that Lawrence had written that the castle was haunted, but by the dogs of the Beri Hillal, the mythical builders of the fort. He said they roamed the six towers each night for their dead masters. It was a passage I had read the previous night. Lawrence heard their wailing too.

'Well, dogs or no dogs, that was definitely the ghost of a man by a wall in that room last night.'

Chapter Seven

Our feelings and thoughts about Lawrence grow day by day. In the beginning we owed our impressions of the man to his writings and to the writings of others who sought to understand his meaning. Ours was a 'paper deduction'.

But now the character behind the mask of controversy is illuminated by the sheer reality of our experience in the desert and our awareness of its secrets and revelations. Its harshness and, above all, the life we are sharing with the Bedouin have enriched our understanding and given colour, sight and sound to the faded black and white picture that, by comparison, is gained from reading *Seven Pillars of Wisdom.* To read it in the comfort of an English home is inadequate, for the complexities of the words and the reader's search for clarity in its twisting sentences are ever more confusing without a knowledge of the land.

Although the armchair reader may find the book romantic, and the descriptions are literary masterpieces, it poses more riddles about Lawrence than it solves. It is, for example, retrospective, self-glorifying and accusingly self-critical. Lawrence's attention was, in the end, not upon the people or the events, but upon himself as a man. In this he was at times extravagant in his own praise, and at other times grossly unjustified in the modesty with which he held his endeavours.

But whatever the impressions, reading such 'art' in isolation from the extra dimension of experience afforded by the Bedouin and the desert itself presents a distorted picture and vilifies the motives of Lawrence.

The confusion is deliberate.

The first sentence of *Seven Pillars* reads: 'Some of the evil of my tale may have been inherent in our circumstances,' a confession not necessarily just about his two years' desert campaigning but perhaps also a clue to the way Lawrence saw his life as a whole. It is as though Lawrence, throughout, never came to terms with what was for him a shattering discovery of a largely non-chivalric world beyond Oxford's walls. And he revelled, masochistically, in the discovery. Pain he made into a challenge; self-doubt into an essential part of his reasoning, a process which guided him along a deeply intellectual path of self-discovery.

He loathed convention and adored to be different. The self-image which he portrayed to his public captured a mood, and he cultivated the legend: 'the inviolate house'. And the legend proliferated and grew increasingly mysterious as readers sought clues to unlock the puzzles he presented in his writings, their arguments serving to fuel the fire of controversy yet further.

Reliving the story on the ground of its making may be illuminating, but the expedition offers no replica to study first-hand the circumstances of the Revolt, no individual answers to his careful intrigue of words. What it does give us is a gradual understanding, an embodiment of the spirit which enabled Lawrence to forge a legend within the span of his short life.

Our main discovery about Lawrence is implicit in our first-hand experience of the Bedouin. Time has exposed this people to Western life and, in particular, to its material possessions. This has removed the strangeness that Lawrence described, but it has not finally altered their nature, their apparent inconsistency, their broad view yet microscopic attention to the detail of every-day life, their sound logic yet child-like naivity. They are a proud people, quick to take offence but do not hold a grudge; they are easily charmed but as easily misunderstood.

On the basis of our experience of the Bedouin nature and temperament, Lawrence's achievement - his success in focusing and maintaining the direction of the Arab Revolt to both Arab and British advantage - is doubly creditable.

Additionally, alongside our doubts expressed earlier about Lawrence's account of his camel's speed, we have been surprised by our discovery of the status accorded to Lawrence's memory in Jordan today. To the Howeitat it is Auda Abu Tayi - not Lawrence - who remains the legendary hero of the Arab Revolt; it is Auda's memory that stirs tribal blood and prompts stories of glorious past deeds. There are those who will respond immediately when Lawrence's name is connected by us with the Revolt, but it appears, at this point in the route, that even among these the memory of Lawrence has been eclipsed by that of Glubb Pasha.

3 March

'Sabaab al-khair.' (Good morning.) 'Sabaab an-noor,' mutters Mohammed as I squat by the fire opposite him. James looks up, nods, and draws on a cigarette while continuing to gaze into the flickering warmth. The dawn is cold, and an imperceptibly thin white veil of mist hangs over the wadi. The camels graze at intervals among the high green shrubs around the pool of water, lowering their heads gracefully, teeth searching among the leaves, and then up come the heads, jaws mechanically crushing and sorting the pickings. They turn to took at us, Barmey stops chewing and then Hashan. Motionless they gaze at us as if forming an opinion. A moment passes and the chewing continues. They turn their heads the other way, and return finally to the shrubs. One eye always appears to be on us. Once in a while a short tail is raised and a wobbly trajectory of hot fluid is ejected to

Refueling the camels at Azraq.

'Of Azraq, as of Rumm, one said "Numen ist." Both were magically haunted: but whereas Rumm was vast and echoing and God-like, Azrak's unfathomable silence was steeped in knowledge of wandering poets, champions, lost kingdoms, all the crime and chivalry and dead magnificence of Hirs and Ghassan. Each stone or blade of it was radiant with half-memory of the luminous silky Eden, which had passed so long ago.' Seven Pillars of Wisdom

the rear, much of it splashing the thighs. The bull camel is one of God's rare creatures whose personal weapon points the wrong way, an affliction which makes it seem partially incontinent.

James breaks the ice in a water carrier, a reminder of the freezing level to which the night temperature drops. He pours some water into the tin bowl and carefully washes the sand from the tea glasses. I have noticed that it is a morning chore everyone avoids since it takes some time to restore circulation to the fingers.

Mohammed coughs, a rasping and unhealthy sound. He spits the phlegm aside and blows his nose by pressing a finger on each nostril in turn. His face is more deeply lined and haggard than I remember noticing before.

'Old Mohammed looks a touch grey this morning, James.' 'Yuh.' 'Yuh! Yuh!' repeats Mohammed, with a mischievous grin. James' habitual sharp intake of breath when he says this is continually imitated by Mohammed.

I walk across the cold sand to wake the others. Their bivvy bags are glazed white with frost. A sharp kick is administered to each, particularly Chris who is the most reluctant riser. He is the first to lay out his sleeping area at the day's end, and the first into his sleeping bag too. Normally the evenings about the fire, talking and laughing over the day's events, are the one time we come together to share experiences and cross the barriers of race and religion. His tendency to opt out and seek the solitude of his bivvy bag annoys me intensely.

I return to the fire where Mohammed has poured the tea. Hamad attends to the feeding and saddling of the camels. Each morning, and following every halt when the baggage is unloaded, the girth and straps of the saddles are checked and adjusted. A camel with a slipping or uncomfortable saddle around its hump will give up and drop heavily to the ground in protest. James lies on his side facing the fire, glass in hand, legs drawn up beneath his robe and the battered toe caps of his black boots protruding. For some time he gazes absent-mindedly into the flames, occasionally scratching what is now a well-formed beard. I ask him what he is thinking about, expecting it to be his girlfriend. To my surprise he tells me it was Napoleon. Continuing to slurp his tea, he explains:

'I was thinking about why he lost Waterloo and what the implications would have been for European history had he not done so. Did you know that one theory was that it was because he had piles?'

'Piles!' I exclaim.

'Yes, and the pain was so great he was confined to a cushioned chair to observe the battle. It affected his decision-making at the crucial moment. Mind you, specimens of his handwriting during the battle are no different to other times, so he couldn't have been in that much discomfort.'

He scratches his beard again and pours more tea for each of us I eye him and smile. Only James could think of Napoleon's piles at 6 am in the middle of a freezing cold desert. I watch the sun rise from behind the uneven horizon, swelling with every second until it escapes to ascend high above the earth in triumphant freedom. It warms the desert from an intensely blue sky and fills our surroundings with colour. I think of it as a sign, a way of reminding us we are not alone in this emptiness. Desert, sky, and sun will complete our company during this Sunday's daylight hours; their interaction alone will shape the thoughts and memories of this camel caravan.

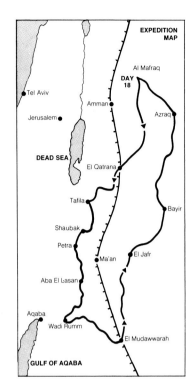

We are grateful at the prospect of another hot day, none of us would welcome a return to the grey sky and strong wind that had heralded our struggle north to Azraq. The individual loads are gathered together and we prepare for another day's travel.

Since departing from Azraq - at dawn on 1 March - we had travelled north-west towards Mushrif: sombre and frustrating miles through a maze of roads, cluttered with fast-moving lorries which reduced our progress to feeble proportions. Our route through Abu Sawana on the first day had been taken by Lawrence in a raid on the railway line from Azraq on 11 November, 1917. He described the action as taking place at the bridge near Minifer, a name we had been unable to locate on the present day maps. We assumed it to be Mushrif. It is now a restricted military area with many bases close to the Syrian border: traditionally a zone of tension, and military alert.

I had been concerned, in the remaining days, to cover the long route south nearer the Dead Sea. With this in mind and tired of restraining frightened camels each time a juggernaut sped past or

The El Qatrana railway
station. Lawrence's legend
was erected upon his exploits
with trains and blowing up
rails. And railways were
never far from Lawrence in
other contexts:

Describing his whipping
at Deraa, 'A hard white
ridge, like a railway,
darkening slowly into
crimson, leaped over my skin
at the instant of each
stroke...'
    And Lawrence lost 'all
but the Introduction and
drafts of Books 9 and 10 at
Reading Station, while
changing trains...'

Below: The day before
reaching El Quatrana we
rest earlier than usual and
our Arabs pray: 'The
Bedouin could not look for
God within him: he was too
sure that he was within
God,' wrote Lawrence.

Above and left *(caravan just visible*, centre*): The descent of Wadi Hesa. On 25 January, 1918, 'the enemy centre was pouring back in disorder through the gap, with our men after them on foot, on horse, on camel,' wrote Lawrence, 'I thought of the depths between here and Kerak, the ravine of Hesa, with its broken, precipitous paths, the undergrowth, the narrows and defiles of the way. It was going to be a massacre and I should have been crying-sorry for the enemy; but after the angers and exertions of the battle my mind was too tired to care to go down into that awful place and spend the night saving them.'

Above right: *The approach to Tafila, 'The only regular set-piece battle Lawrence was involved in during the war.'*

Right: *The village of Hauf on the way to Petra.*
   Twilight of 9 March: 'The village turns out to be no more than half-a-dozen old mud and stone-walled houses...that nestle into the rock-face...Sounds of bleating goats, the odd metallic bang, the cry of a baby, and some indiscernible Arab talk is suspended on the still, cold night-air.'

Left: *Petra - 'There is virtual silence as the rocks on either side close in, and we ride along the narrow Syk, the walls of which are hundreds of feet high. Here it is cool, the only light coming from the small opening to the sky far above; sometimes the rock almost meets overhead. The twisting passage is along a large fissure in the rock formation, and through this opening (only 6 feet wide in places) we guide our camels... Some birds are calling high above us and I catch the odd glimpse of them as they flit between the rock ledges and the little greenery that clings to the steep sides.'*

Below: *'The Palace Tomb, its two entrances leading to chambers carefully shaped into large square rooms. The man who owns it invites our party to be his guests for a mensaff and to spend the night.'*

a military jet screamed overhead, we had turned towards El Qatrana and the void swallowed us once more - a blissful retreat into the silence of the desert.

The Bedu were happy to know they were returning home, and the camels moved quickly after the rest at Azraq. Things have improved, psychologically, since Mohammed joked that the camels could smell Wadi Rumm and, if allowed to go free, would make their own return journey home.

With their loading complete, I spread the map across Hashan's saddle, note the contours of the jebel, fix a bearing with the Silva compass, and satisfied with the route, prepare to mount. Normally the camels are walked for the first two hours but I have ridden much of the route since Azraq in an attempt to ease the pain in my roughly bandaged foot. A large splinter of wood had penetrated the sole of my left foot through open sandals, causing it to swell and become septic. After a quick check of the camp site we move off towards the undulating hills.

It is a splendid morning, the caravan moving with professional ease: outwardly, it seems, Arabs and English are now as one. But in spite of Hamad's preparations, the load and saddle slips on Chris's camel. We have travelled only five minutes...this is becoming too frequent a frustration. Mohammed sits by some brushwood, lights a cigarette and watches Hamad, taking no interest in the remaining five camels. All are Hamad's concern, which he takes seriously, fussing over the speed we ride and forever drawing our attention to some isolated shrub to quell their hunger. Mohammed cares only for his son's camel, which gives Mark reason to think it very spoilt and enjoy flicking its rear with his riding stick when Mohammed is not looking.

Hamad takes his time, soothing the camel with a continual 'Kh-Kh-Kh-Kh' while carefully readjusting the saddle. He finishes loading and prepares to leave.

Suddenly Mohammed yells, tugs hard on his rein and walks deliberately towards Hamad. They stand shouting loudly at each other from either side of the nervously couched animal. Mohammed aggressively unloads the sacks of grain again from their loops over the pommels and dumps them on the ground. Tugging at the saddle straps he re-positions it on the folded rug over the hump. Hamad throws up his hands in despair, cursing and shouting.

We are baffled. The argument, a torrent of Arabic, continues as the confused animal is loaded a third time, Mohammed moving to Hamad's side and correcting his work. Finally Mohammed looks to us, says Hamad knows nothing of camels and stalks off in a rage. I study Hamad. He looks hurt and mumbles to himself as he checks the baggage of his own mount, crestfallen at the blow his pride has taken in front of us. We have grown fond of his gentle ways, like a true Bedouin he is devoted to his camels' needs before his own. More recently, too, Hamad has sided with us during Mohammed's unpredictable tantrums, causing Chris to name them respectively, 'the faithful' and 'the obstinate'.

We head south, Hamad sulking to the rear, stumbling along in an exaggerated shamble.

Mohammed is of the warrior caste - quick in tongue and mind - and is still, at times, unreasonably awkward. But now, when he shouts to Chris or Mark about their camels or a trivial thing around the camp fire, I intervene and remind him that he is our chief handler only. We remain locked in this constant clash of personalities...a continual strain.

As ever we travel in silence, each man sunk in thought. The halts are the main chances for communication, and I wonder at our increasing insularity - whether the unchanging scene and established routines are making us shrink into ourselves.

We are moving up a gradual incline, the camels nimbly picking their way in spite of their large frames, when Hamad rides up to attract my attention. I know what he wants to talk about, so for a while I concentrate on my balance and steer Hashan to where the loose rocks are more thinly spread. Finally, unable to ignore Hamad any longer, I respond to his gesture to drop further behind the others, who now move ahead in single file along a narrow defile that opens onto a sandy plain.

While watching the back of Mohammed, he pours out his complaints: Mohammed is a bad man, Mohammed does not understand camels, his navigation adds unnecessary miles to each daily ride, he is wanting money all the time... There is little to say in reply, though Hamad looks at me, searching for reassurance.

In poor Arabic I tell him he is a good man and good with camels. It consoles him. I feel placed in an awkward position with a man much older than myself but with half my mental age. Worse still he smiles and thanks me profusely. My glib tongue and Hamad's gullibility remind me of Lawrence's own feeling that he was deceiving the Arabs.

Navigation is difficult, the map a maze of brown contours and broken blue lines of wadis - the desert watercourses, all dried up. The desert is in its third metamorphosis. Since Rumm it has gone from fine sand to black flint and now to a strange undulating terrain. Its colour is not dissimilar to a patchy piece of burnt toast, shades of brown sand and rock with large areas of small black boulders, together almost as though arranged that way by someone. In other places the rich yellow sand is a vivid contrast to sharp volcanic waste, an effect interesting to the eye at close range but hypnotically plain as unending panorama.

It is 11.30. We stop to allow James time to complete a noon-hour sun fix and calculate our exact position. For once Mohammed wishes to continue further, and this new enthusiasm to maximise the hours of travel appears as yet another feature in his unpredictability. I dwell more and more on Hamad's words.

It is a frustrating mental battle to follow Mohammed's moods; our understanding of simple things is so different that I wonder how Lawrence coped with more than one Mohammed among his party. Perhaps it explains the extent of his mental exhaustion following the two years of campaigning and manipulation of Arab leaders in the Revolt. My battle is with one man, and after little more than two weeks it is quite a test of leadership. Moreover I can find respite in the company of fellow Englishmen; for Lawrence there was seldom that opportunity.

Three of the camels wander far from where we are. They skip like kangaroos, their front legs tied tightly together with rope, as they seek better grazing. It is ridiculous to watch, and their awkwardness is a major source of amusement. Mohammed sends Hamad to bring them back. Obediently he leaves his tea and heads off, doing so with a smile, resigned to the inconvenience because everything is the work of Allah. It occurs to me that he probably does not regard Mohammed's words as an order, or that he is the lesser of the two in status; it is part of his way of life and he simply knows no other.

'Hamad no good,' says Mohammed once the shambling figure is far enough away. I do not ask why. I know Mohammed will continue without encouragement.

'Hamad want money money...he know nothing of camel. Ham is bad man and lazy man.' He clicks his tongue in disapproval. The rivalry between the two amuses us, a pantomime to reflect on in quiet moments and lighten the days' monotony. It began after Bayir, each conspiring against the other when his back was turned, an ocean of little intrigues as each seeks to elevate himself in our estimation.

This is both a recent and novel development. In the early days of the expedition, it had been very much the Englishmen and the Arabs - the former particularly self-conscious, unsure of themselves and, as a result, allowing much of the flow of events to be taken out of their hands. Now, my leadership is established more certainly, and so the Arabs have begun to channel their needs through me as opposed to sorting things out between themselves.

The afternoon sun burns our faces and dries the skin as we ride south. Mohammed catches me applying some Nivea cream which causes tremendous amusement. But the laughter and teasing once more unites us and there are no rifts, no tension, and no resentment of cruel words spoken indiscreetly in the past. I watch the two Bedu ride together sharing the humour of English soldiers behaving as women with all their creams. It is as though they are brothers, and I wonder again at this Arab ability to remain so intimate despite differences and insults.

Mohammed laughs loudly, and proudly claims James to be the only man among us, the only Bedouin of the English, since he prefers never to clean himself or use any sun creams. 'Madame! Madame!' exclaims Mohammed loudly and looks at me with a wicked grin. I know I cannot help but like him, somehow. Even the camels appear to feel the relaxed atmosphere, treading more carefully as we ride the flat plain, the sun setting to our right.

The ground is neither sandy nor rocky, rather a fine dried brown clay out of which grow wisps of green grass. To either side are low hills which seem to preserve this sacred spot in its vivid evening colour. Ahead are clumps of green tamarisk following the line of a thin gulley. I tell Mohammed to make camp there, and the camels stretch their long necks forward towards the smell of water and abundant grazing. But we bypass what appears to be the best spot.

Again I tell Mohammed to camp in the area, he in turn confers with Hamad as they search it with their eyes. We continue to ride.

Chris and Mark are to the rear trying to understand how the Bedouin choose a site. It has baffled us in the past and we have tried to come to terms with the inconsistency of their choice. There are few common factors. After much discussion between the Bedu we do eventually halt. I had assumed grazing for the camels to be the main priority - yet this site has little to offer. The camels are couched and hobbled in an uncomfortably rocky area where they remain, and we have to forage far afield for suitable brushwood. Mark continues to wonder why the Bedouin selected such an obviously bad place, but it remains yet another anomaly in our dealings with them.

It is now 7.30 pm. There is a cloudless sky and complete silence, broken only by a bird calling across the wadi that sounds similar to a nightjar. James and I have just completed a star fix using Cirus, Regulus and Duhbe - it is the second take since he got Duhbe in the wrong position originally. He lies by the firelight calculating it all, and I am concerned that the result be accurate since the contours of the jebel confuse all estimates of our position.

Mohammed and I had a blinding row earlier over such a trivial thing; Mark had placed a soup bowl incorrectly on the fire. But the argument stemmed, indirectly, from his behaviour this evening. He had sat down and curled up in his sheepskin coat as soon as we made camp, and done nothing to assist in collecting firewood or feeding the camels. I took the opportunity to have a go at him, particularly since recently he has contributed less and less to the team effort. The net result is that he is now sulking, not eating or talking. As he has begun to annoy all of us I do not feel guilty.

4 March

Mohammed squats by the gulley and retches loudly. He is pitiful in his sickness. For the first time I see him as he is, a middle-aged man who has endured a life of uninterrupted harshness; he returns to where we wait by the camels, who shiver along with him in the cold morning air. His face is pale, his eyes downcast with suffering; gone are the jokes, the commands, the flaring temper and the laughter. Mohammed is a sick man.

He stands before me with a moving dependence, seeking my help and searching my face with his eyes as if I have a cure. He complains of chest pains and difficulty in breathing, muttering that he did not sleep during the night. Chris hands him some Paracetamol which he takes with meek acceptance.

What concern I feel is expressed, perhaps more callously, in a quip from Mark who says he hopes Mohammed doesn't have a heart attack and die on us. The illness is a problem. We are miles from anywhere and our medical pack and training is fairly limited. There is no alternative but to continue on towards El Qatrana where at least a doctor might be found if the illness persists.

Hamad takes the reins of both camels and leads off, leaving Mohammed walking alone, arms folded across his body, shivering uncontrollably.

'Mind you, if he does snuff it at least there'll be more grub for each of us,' Mark continues.

We walk slowly, Hamad at the front suddenly in command, selecting the route which we follow in single file. I concentrate on the map and compass, happy for the first time with James' star fix which had pinpointed our wadi beyond doubt.

Overhead two Egyptian vultures, beautiful in their precise black and white markings against the clear blue sky, silently circle the caravan for some while. They are the first large birds we have seen.

'Reckon they're waiting for Mohammed to drop by the wayside?' says Chris with a backwards glance to the vulnerable looking figure at the rear.

'Nah!' replies Mark, 'He's all skin and bone anyway!'

Such jibes have become more frequent from Mark and show his growing confidence with the Bedouin as much as his own brand of humour. He is now at ease with his surroundings and contains situations with his down-to-earth Birmingham logic. In turn, his stumpy plod of a walk is a source of amusement for Mohammed. His robe has been split lengthways to allow a longer stride and give more freedom of movement whilst riding; the kaffiyah he wears wrapped around his neck. With sleeves rolled up high, black beard and white chubby face despite the sun, he looks anything other than a seasoned desert traveller. James had remarked once that if he had to picture a 'Brummy' lad in the desert then Mark was what he would expect. With little previous travelling experience, his observations of Bedouin mannerisms and moods is acute. He meets them and us squarely as Arabs and officers, unfettered by convention.

Chris, by comparison, develops in a way known to himself alone. Sensitive amid the harsh life, strong and capable, frequently quiet and retiring, he remains shyly uncertain about

Mohammed's verbal assaults. My extrovert nature resents this withdrawal. The knife he carries is continually cleaned and sharpened, the clothes he wears well arranged, and his countenance always clean and fresh. His detached, self-contained, anonymous behaviour is frustrating to me. Nevertheless a quiet strength can be sensed in his athletic and suntanned body. A typical Teutonic embodiment of youth. Again I am reminded of Lawrence's observation when he wrote, 'Stokes, the Englishman, was driven by the Arab strangeness to become more himself, more insular. His shy correctness reminded my men in every movement that he was unlike them, and English.'

It is only James I feel I really know.

We rest earlier than usual, for Mohammed's sake. The pains in his chest persist, and again he moves away to be sick alone. As Chris opens the medical pack to give Mohammed Paracetemol, he looks on like a dependant child, perhaps half expecting an instant cure to appear. It is sad to watch the force and strength of his personality dwindle before us. The sickness shrivels him as though he has suddenly aged twenty years. The dominating, extrovert character is replaced by vulnerability. It is a situation we try not to exploit, recognizing his right to suffer alone without betraying any sign of weakness.

In spite of the warmth from the sun, he wraps his sheepskin coat about him, and collecting the grain sacks for pillows, lies down to sleep. Hamad tends the camels. We strip off, apply lotions, and stretch out to enjoy an hour's sun-bathing. Only James is fully clothed - heavy boots on - and remarks that there is nothing more contemptible than an Englishman sun-bathing. 'If God had wanted you to be brown he would have made you that way. It smells like a beach on Costa del Sol round here!' he mutters, and settles to read his copy of the *Koran*.

He had brought the book on the expedition as his 'sole companion', somewhat idealistically intending to read it in an attempt, through their own literature, to understand the Arab world, their beliefs and the basis of their religion. But this is only the second time I have seen him produce it.

I had also left England clutching a book, a collection of poetry from Shakespeare through to Rupert Brooke and Robert Graves, which I too had had visions of reading at length, exploring the beauty of words beneath the countless stars of the Arabian sky.

The need to travel light had restricted us to one book each (besides the dictionary and *Seven Pillars*, which I excused as essential expedition equipment), and though we had not spoken of them before departure we had both regarded our selected works as special means of mental stimulus appropriate to our surroundings. We had assumed there would be long spells of boredom and idleness in the desert, occasions that our conversations or private thoughts would not fill.

But my poetry remains unopened. We were wrong on all

counts. The daily existence and length of time spent travelling provide no opportunity for reading. The nights are too cold and our bodies too aching and exhausted to appreciate more scholarly pursuits. Each man eats, rides, thinks and speaks as one of six travelling companions - there is no time to be alone. Furthermore the monotony and drudgery of this harsh journey saps our patience, alters our perspectives and leaves us silent creatures amongst it all, grimly persevering with the daily routine, dulled by its repetition and our growing familiarity with the novelties of the early days. For their part, the Bedu cannot even understand a man's desire to write a daily diary in private - what could we be writing about, and why? Their way of life precludes any respect for an individual's 'peace and quiet' moods.

Lawrence carried but one book throughout his time in the desert. It was Malory's *Morte d'Arthur*. As I lie on the hard ground gazing into the depths of the blue sky, I wonder on how many occasions he found the peace to read.

Indifferent to the sand and the heat I roll to one side, prop myself up and survey the scene. The camels have wandered far and are barely discernable against the intense glare of our sur-roundings - everything is a brilliant white yellow as the rocks and sand reflect the sun's rays. There is no cover or protection from the heat, and foolishly, in our lethargy, we lie exposed to it, our sweat cleansing the dirty pores in our skin.

Our thobes are white with dust from contact with the ground, and numerous small burn marks on the front bear witness to times spent around desert fires sparking in the wind. We are dirty, bearded, sweaty and smelly but no longer find it uncomfor-table - it is impossible to be otherwise, especially with the camels, and besides, our Bedouin have not washed for these nineteen days. A pressing lack of water due to the loss of considerable quantities from leaking containers and evaporation beneath the full force of the sun, has prevented it. I drink a little from a carrier beside me, it is hot and hardly thirst quenching. My injured foot throbs painfully...

All of a sudden Hamad catches my attention; he is carefully washing his feet and hands in our communal eating bowl. Unsure of this latest extravagance and, through weariness, indifferent to its consequences, I continue simply to observe him. He pours the precious water over his feet, stands up and moves a little way to be alone. Kneeling down he removes the band of his headdress, places it aside, and stares fervently into the middle distance. Suddenly I realise he is about to pray, and that washing himself was in preparation for this.

Mohammed had told me once that he does not pray daily because he cannot make himself clean. Had they both been able to, perhaps we would have no water left at all! Nevertheless, having been together in the desert some while, I am surprised not to have witnessed our Bedouin praying more often. Abdulla did not pray once in the eight days he accompanied us, and of them all it is Hamad who appears the most devout. Taking the Silva compass I check exactly which way he faces; it is south, the direction of Mecca. His body is relaxed as he sits on his heels, hands clasped loosely together, head bowed and lips moving silently in prayer. He bends forward to touch the ground with his head, simultaneously stretching his arms upwards and outwards in offering. He stands quickly, crosses his head and chest with one hand and talks aloud. The expression on his face is simple and sincere. It is as though he has mortally offended Allah, and the sins and cares of the caravan are his entire responsibility. Several times he repeats the sequence of standing, kneeling and bowing forwards to the ground, continually repeating his prayers and the name of Allah, his god. It is a moving scene. I want to take a photograph but feel reluctant to invade his privacy at this moment. He prays for five minutes. When he has finished I notice the imprint of sand on his forehead and a line of it along the bridge of his nose.

From where he lies, Mohammed also watches. As though spurred on by Hamed's example, he rises and attends to washing himself too. Moving away from our camp he stands, facing more to the south-east. I check my watch. It is 12 am, the hour every devout Moslem in the land must pray to Allah. Mohammed's worship is different. He retains an air of dignity and his prayer appears less passionate or devout. He does not bend forward to touch the ground with his head, but prefers to stand and pray with head bowed and hands clasped in front. My impression is that Mohammed is merely going through the motions, whereas Hamad is the true believer.

When it is over I join them both by the grey embers of the fire. We drink the last of the tea together. Mohammed seems better and I mention their praying to try and draw him into conversation. I ask why it is that Hamad faces one way, Mohammed the other, and why the difference in the time of their worship. Mohammed laughs and says that Hamad has no watch and therefore does not know when it is exactly 12.00. Mohammed shows his own watch with a chuckle and taps his head knowingly. He winks and smiles craftily. This is more the Mohammed we know and admire. Hamad replies that since he has no watch he must be very clever to calculate the time for prayer from the sun and his own shadow. The direction they face is not resolved. It pleases me to listen to their chatter as they take good-humoured digs at each other. Mohammed claims that Hamad is a little simple, more of a peasant Bedouin, and so his mistakes are understandable. Hamad shows no resentment.

We left the jebel around late afternoon. My diary entry reads: 'During the afternoon I lost a section of the map for the second time and it must have fallen from my saddle bag while riding. Leaving the others I retraced my route and searched for three hours on foot, covering about 5 miles on my own. The wind had obviously blown it far away.

'I felt quite weak from the extra exertion of searching for the map when we camped in a wide wadi which leads to the plain and El Qatrana. Tonight, as we sat around the fire and the night grew colder, we heard our first hyenas. Later we saw one on a far ridge silhouetted in the moonlight. The Bedouin brought the camels in closer and packed the food well into the centre of our camp. The last time I had heard hyenas was whilst trekking alone in the Himalayas. They have an eerie presence.'

5 March

We reach the town of El Qatrana in the late morning, which lies in a dust bowl at the foot of the jebel. It has a railway station built by the Turks (later captured by the Arab army), as the Hejaz line runs through it and on down to El Mudawwarah.

The town is filthy, particularly on the outskirts, with shacks of cardboard, flattened tin and boxes, and dirty, skinny stray dogs wandering hungrily among the refuse. We pick our way through empty cans, glass and old wire as we approach the station from the desert. The rusted railway lines are full of rolling stock and an old steam engine, none of it operational.

After the cleanliness and peace of the desert it is no pleasure to reach this 'go-between' shanty town. Of its inhabitants, many have never even seen a camel, and the elders must have felt nostalgic as they watched us reliving the traditional Bedouin way of life. Now that they have left their goat-hair tents to move to the towns, much of their dignity and old values in life have gone too. We feel like time travellers between two cultures.

We buy 4 kilos of sheeps' meat for 10 Jordanian Dinas (approximately £20) at the 'Butchers' (it is no more than a chopping block in the dusty street). There is a skinned sheep dangling from a hook which is chopped up for us. A rather sorry looking sheep, tethered to the same block, looks on, obviously wondering when it is to share the same fate as a friend who was alive only this morning.

Happily leaving the bustle of El Qatrana behind, we ride south following the Hejaz railway for a while before cutting west across the desert towards the Wadi Hesa. From there we will pick up one of Lawrence's mapped routes through Tafilia, Shaubak, Abu el Lassan and finally to Aqaba. Sadly the route will be through well-inhabited towns and villages until the Guweria plain is reached, north of Wadi Rumm. Our isolation is nearly at an end.

This evening, for the first time on this journey, we go to our sleeping bags with full stomachs. Hamad cooked the sheep on the charcoal, and we relished our only meat in two weeks (all except Chris, that is). With fresh bread and the luxury of sufficient water for two pots of tea, we have feasted well. The distant drone of lorries on the main Amman to Aqaba highway, and the glowing horizon of a reflected town's lights, remind us that the sanctuary of the desert is no more.

6 March

It is 6 am as we skirt the fringes of the hill village of Mkar. There is a gentle frost everywhere and we wear our sweatshirts to offset the dawn chill. A shepherd boy leads his goats up the dusty trail to our front, their neck bells a delightfully clear sound as they move with an irregular trot.

'Do you know why they paint their doors and windows blue?' asks James. 'It's something I learnt in the Sinai, apparently they believe it will prevent evil coming into the house, and as the Devil flies along he sees the blue doors and windows, thinks they are part of the sky, and moves on to another house.'

I take the conversation no further as I am obsessed with calculating the speed of our journey south, and the need to reach Tafila by dusk. It has become the single most tiring aspect of leading the expedition. The constant worry and strain of reaching our objectives on time result in frustration and anger as the sedate speed of the camel seems to work against our success.

It is difficult to control the urge to push ahead quickly, to cover a particular stretch of ground and look expectantly over a distant hill line, though often we would only see an exact replica of the previous few miles and no discernable landmark.

My other thoughts concern the expedition's British members. Without ever intending it two factions have emerged. I am conscious of my close rapport with James and of how he serves as a confidant in the many problems over the Bedouin, camels, and the route to be taken. Because of our long-standing friendship and similar interests I turn to him for opinion and support and we examine and analyse the Bedouin life together, often and unintentionally to the exclusion of Mark and Chris. Although the relationship between the four of us is easy and relaxed, I am aware that I should rely less on James and more on the others in order to increase their participation in everday events.

For over three hours we twist our way through the wadis, trying to offset the struggle of ascending and descending every hill in between. The morning becomes very hot and I am annoyed at the time it takes to cover a short distance. Still the map shows nothing other than closely packed brown contour lines. On the ground, low hills fold into each other with interlocking irregularity, their tightness barring easy passage and forcing us to contour the rounded and boulder-strewn bottoms in our struggle to work our way south-west.

I realise I am totally lost, and Mohammed fares no better. He turns and asks which way the compass tells us to go (following our heated arguments en route to Jafr this is quite an admission).

James with the Silva compass.

'"Boosalla mush ques," scoffs Mohammed as he turns his back and walks on assuming he is right.'

When I reply, he dutifully heads that way with no argument. Fortunately his health seems to have improved, and I was relieved we lost no time in El Qatrana on account of it.

The gulley widens. We ascend the side of a small hill to where wadis and gullies have formed on a different, higher level. I look back towards Mkar, an old wind pump marking its distant position. In two hours we have turned full circle.

I fume, and my discomfort at our wasted hours increases with the morning heat. I feel trapped amid the maze of undulating hills, the surface rock a barren grey and yellow, sharp, ugly and barely touched by the eroding wind. Even small tufts of hard scrub, dried and paled by the sun, clinging stubbornly in their solitary existence, manage to add a little colour to this desolate patchwork of ground.

As we move on, we come across a Bedouin family still in the process of establishing itself, a large goat-hair tent spread on the ground in sections, and piles of domestic utensils scattered indiscriminately. Two women - mother and daughter, we presume - unravel the guy ropes of the tent, and the man carries large sacks from an old tractor. A small child plays with a stick, rattling it backwards and forwards against wooden crates of chickens. There are no other livestock, no camels. Perhaps they will arrive later.

We decide to rest awhile, allowing our camels to graze, and watch. The man approaches and invites Mohammed to drink tea with him. In turn Mohammed asks me, but seeing their fire is not yet lit, I decline. I know how long it will take to begin the process, to roast and pound coffee beans, before the tea stage is even reached. I also know that in their eyes I am being rude to refuse, but it is only the need to exploit every daylight hour which urges me forwards.

Fortunately Mohammed appears indifferent and accepts my decision. When he manages to explain my position, the man implores us to stay. Mohammed repeats the invitation, but once more I state we must get on to Tafila. In the Bedouin world it is almost unheard of to pass a tent and refuse the invitation of hospitality. As Mohammed asks directions for our route, I begin to notice the young girl as she moves gracefully and unhurriedly around the tent. I try to work out her age, comparing her to her mother, who looks toughened and weathered by the life. The girl's long black robe catches tightly around her behind as she bends, and I glimpse her beautiful compact figure. She continues her work, shyly aware of our stares, occasionally smiling and making comments to her mother.

'You know that they say if you admire something of theirs, they are obliged to give it to you?' remarks Mark, catching my look.

'Yes.'

'Well, why don't you openly admire his daughter and perhaps he will present you with a bride!' We all laugh. I realise it is the first time I have looked at a young woman for three weeks, and this native girl distracts my mind refreshingly from more serious thoughts.

'Perhaps we should stay for lunch,' says Chris, 'you can see she fancies you!'

'I hardly think so,' I reply, good-humouredly.

Wearily we move again, Mohammed heading directly south. When I tell him we must continue south-west he replies that the Bedouin gave the directions. By the position of the water pump it does seem that we are virtually on our original track. But, suppressing any doubts, I allow Mohammed to lead, hoping that his route will indeed see the caravan across Wadi Hesa and into Tafila by nightfall. In shaa Allah.

We walk for one hour, with barely any discernible progress. Cresting the ridge in front, we are stopped dead in our tracks by the sight that unfolds before us. It is utterly unexpected. We stand and stare, awe-struck by the sudden revelation of this vast, hidden entity.

After weeks of the same flat desert, to stand on the hill and gaze at the Wadi Hesa is a stunning experience. My geography remains confused, but now it lies before us like a great divide. We cannot see the other side - there is none! As though slashed, deeply, several times by a mighty sword, the ground before us extends in giant cuts towards a lazy horizon, bare rock with black lines of strata, rounded hillocks and razor sharp ridges, and vertical plunges to an unseen wadi bottom.

We contour a steep-sided hill and follow an animal trail which leads towards the wadi. The hill in front dominates our caravan - the lines of hard rock strata curving with its own shape, as though streaks of chocolate in a whipping bowl of cream. It takes half an hour's descent to reach the edge of the wadi: more a line of rock, below which the ground drops over 1,500 feet, and beyond which it is divided into vast valleys for a width of over 2 miles.

It appears impassable. There are no visible tracks and the landscape, which looks like a smaller version of the Grand Canyon, is I conclude beyond our camels' physical capability. Consulting the map I approximate our position. The Wadi Hesa extends east-west for some 40 miles, draining into the Dead Sea at its western end. It seems that we have struck it too far east. The alternative to crossing directly is to parallel it towards the Dead Sea and cross at a more accessible point near the route to Tafila. I explain my plan to Mohammed.

He smiles.

'Mohammed, go straight, go straight,' he chants, imitating my usual instruction to him, which just as often he has ignored. I understand little more of what he says, but enough to know that he thinks the best route is straight ahead, and that he cannot see why I should want to do a Mohammed-style detour.

The twinkle in his eye shows he is going to enjoy it. Looking

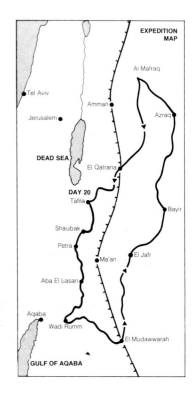

The descent of Wadi Hesa.

'I thought of the depths between here and Kerak, the ravine of Hesa, with its broken, precipitous paths, the undergrowth, the narrows and defiles of the way...' Seven Pillars of Wisdom

'The whole expedition was very lucky as we had no real physical injury, when by rights there should have been. If anything had happened I don't think we'd have been fit to cope, there was no way we could have contacted anyone.'

again at the depth and width of the wadi I decide to throw the decision open to the others.

Either way it is a long and tiring route, that is true. Our final decision is that Mohammed is seldom wrong, and that crossing the wadi presents the expedition with a challenge at least. So, we decide to go straight. Mohammed laughs at our trepidation as he begins to lead us directly downwards.

'Quite typical of the Arab mentality, James,' I remark, 'the only time the old rogue decides to go in a straight line is across a maze of mini-Grand Canyons, 2 miles wide and 1,500 feet deep!'

'And you're complaining?' he jokes.

Secretly I am impressed. Only Hamad objects, fearing the effects of such a journey on the camels. We stop to check their loads. The saddle straps are tightened, some weight redistributed and the balance of the baggage of each animal is checked carefully. Mohammed tells us to keep a close tight rein on our animals.

Mohammed leads with Hamad at the rear - an even distribution of expertise in the event of a crisis. I give my camel to Hamad in order to photograph the descent. With nothing more than two cameras slung around my neck, and my riding stick in hand, I feel gloriously free.

The descent begins. It is slow, clumsy and painstaking work and each camel is coaxed gently along. Rocks slip and tumble downwards, small avalanches of boulders cascade to the bottom. Mohammed selects his own route, 's'-bending to and fro across the strata and loose boulders. I take some pictures, and look down to see brushwood in the wadi bottom.

The danger is mainly for the animals. One slip would take them and their load crashing hundreds of feet below. The rock face is near vertical. I would not believe it to be possible for the camels, heavily laden as they are, to nimbly inch their way down it.

It is very hot and there is no wind. No one talks. The concentration is intense, each man totally involved in easing his beast slowly along the safe route. The camels do not look downwards, trusting their riders who cling tightly to the reins and soothe and coax them on.

The trail is sharp with flint boulders. The soft hoofs of the camels become deeply cut and bloodied as their legs straighten sharply outwards to correct a loss of balance. Hamad becomes agitated and shouts excitedly at Mark, who is leading Barmey with a loose rein. The large camel is having the greatest difficulty, taking each step haltingly, hoofs searching empty air before locating a foothold, and then skidding on a scree of loose boulders while lunging with his other feet to correct his balance.

It is unnerving to watch. At any moment I expect a disaster.

Slowly the caravan progresses. Each bend leading to lower ground turns into a repetition of the higher path. Suddenly Barmey halts and refuses to move, his front legs pushed obstinately outwards, his long neck straining against Mark's insistent tugging. Hamad shouts and Mohammed stops to look up. Barmey is perched in a precarious position on a small ledge of rock. Insensitively Mark hits the camel with his riding stick to urge him on. Barmey jumps in response and begins to overbalance; the load appears to slip, and showers of rock scatter below as the camel's feet search in panic for a firm footing. Everyone watches helplessly. My heart races as I foresee the possible outcome, and still Barmey bucks and kicks as he seeks firmer rock.

At length he succeeds, but only just - his hoofs bloody from his efforts. The caravan closes up - Barmey had faltered because there was no camel in front of him. Hamad is convinced that one of them will soon plunge to its death. Still the camels are nursed gingerly down the wadi side, and I am amazed at their agility.

Gratefully we reach a levelling of the slope and gaze back in astonishment at the vertical rock face. Then we look into the broad, wide basin of the wadi - a greying-sand colour, shot through with the deep blue line of a stream, and speckled with the green of innumerable bushes. It is the most luxuriant sight of our long journey.

Yet the descent is to be still harder. A few hundred feet below, the slope broadens and then widens into a tongue of grey rock completely different to the rest. Fine and smooth looking, there are no sharp rocks on its surface, but it drops vertically with even less chance of footholds.

The point is reached safely. I scout ahead seeking a route to

complete the last couple of hundred feet to the bottom. Mohammed joins me. We now see that the tongue of rock we stand on has
deep gulleys either side extending far into the mountain, almost
to our starting point. The gulleys themselves are too steep and
narrow for the camels; but if there is no way down we will have to
make a substantial detour.

We are very thirsty, hot and dusty. The lice crawl abou. us in
droves. The feet of the camels bleed badly, and Hamad complains about Mohammed's route and the ridiculous position to
which it has led us. Mohammed ignores him and searches further
afield for a way down. Some way to the right I find a likely spot.
Mohammed does not trust it and prefers to take the camels up the
opposite gulley and around - a long and tiring journey. He leads
off and I choose my own path in order to photograph their
progress. After some difficulty I reach the wadi bottom. It is a sun
trap. I run to the far side to view the caravan, putting up a
partridge from the shade of a large bush as I go.

It is some time before I see them, moving along the wadi side
and descending at a gentle angle. I photograph them at leisure,
more than grateful not to have my patience tested in leading
Hashan over such arduous ground. Finally the caravan rests in
the bottom of Wadi Hesa. The descent has taken three hours, the
hoofs of three of the camels have been injured, and all of them are
exhausted: a white and yellow phlegm covers some of their
mouths after vomiting from their exertions.

We strip off completely to enjoy a long rest. Hamad says the
camels are finished and can go no further. Interestingly Mohammed ignores him, jokingly telling me our way out is directly up
the far side. I grimace, scratch my lice-irritated skin and absent-
mindedly note that this is one of the most interesting features of
our journey - not as regards Lawrence, but for sheer endurance.

I collect my few washing things and head to the running water
to take a first wash in three weeks. My hair is matted, dusty and
tangled, my feet grazed and pitted by exposure to the wind and
sand, and my body foul smelling as well as lice ridden.

Mohammed is already there. He stands completely naked in the
water lathering his body with soap, and with his skinny arms and
legs he reminds me more of a character in a Giles cartoon than a
desert warrior.

He has removed his headdress and for the first time I notice he
is bald apart from a fringe of grey hair. He smiles without a trace
of self-consciousness. The water is dark brown and freezing cold.
It bites at my skin making it tingle, and my head is numbed with
the chill. It is invigorating and I bathe for some while.

I am reminded of Lawrence's own experience in the waterfall
above the settlement at Rumm. It is the one desert bath he
describes in *Seven Pillars of Wisdom:* 'Upon the water-cleansed and
fragrant ledge I undressed my soiled body, and stepped into the
little basin, to taste at last a freshness of moving air and water

against my tired skin. It was deliciously cool. I lay there quietly, letting the clear, dark red water run over me in a ribbly stream, and rub the travel-dirt away.'

Sitting by the fire later, drinking some tea, the initial joy of our bathing is not sustained. Dressing in the same dirty clothes had been tolerable until the vermin began to feed afresh on my cleansed skin. The irritation and itching is greater than ever. We all suffer it. James curses. He had intended to stay as he was until I persuaded him otherwise, saying how pleasant it was, and that it was just what Lawrence had done. The Bedouin sleep.

It is 3 pm and I know we must leave the wadi soon or remain for the night. The temptation is strong to rest in this paradise of water and greenery, but, as ever, I fear dropping too far behind on our schedule. The vertical south side of the wadi towering above us, hundreds of feet away, reminds me that we are but half way. The descent of Wadi Hesa and the swim in its water had been the most exhilarating moment of our journey, but as with everything in the desert, moments of contentment are very short lived. Always there is the threat of an even greater hurdle around the corner.

'Next day, in the early heat, we were near Guweira,' wrote Lawrence about 8 September, 1917, 'comfortably crossing the sanded plain of restful pink with its grey-green undergrowth, when there came a droning through the air. Quickly we drove the camels off the open road into the bush-speckled ground... We waited there, soberly, in the saddle while our camels grazed the little which was worth eating in the scrub, until the aeroplane had circled twice about the rock of Guweira in front of us, and planted three loud bombs.'

Above: *Our last night in the desert, the overhang of this mushroom-shaped rock was blackened by Bedouin fires of the past.* Left, *our final meal, Mohammed smoking my father's Kaywoodie pipe.*

Right, *an earlier picture, taken by Bill Lyons, outside El Mureigha when Mohammed (first left) threw one of his tantrums. 'Despite the exasperation of his moods, Mohammed had guided us caringly through a great deal. Mohammed was Mohammed the whole time, it was I who changed...the expedition was made by the personality of the man.'*

Above: *The final ride to Rumm - 'There were no footmarks on the ground, for each wind swept like a great brush over the sand surface, stippling the traces of the last travellers till the surface was again a pattern of innumerable tiny virgin waves.'* Seven Pillars of Wisdom

Above: *Mohammed's tent, and,* below: *back home in London. 'In my case, the efforts... to live in the dress of Arabs, and to imitate their mental foundation, quitted me of my English self, and let me look at the West and its conventions with new eyes: they destroyed it all for me. At the same time I could not sincerely take on the Arab skin: it was an affectation only...'* Seven Pillars of Wisdom

Chapter Eight

7 March

Our first glimpse of the snow on the mountains is ominous - after recently enjoying the heat again, we dread the cold conditions we soon expect to meet. It lies on the highest peaks of the range of hills which runs parallel to the Wadi Arabah and the Dead Sea to the west. Once we reach Tafila our route will take us south to Aqaba through the highest part of Jordan.

Since crossing the Wadi Hesa yesterday, which took a lot out of the camels, particularly the ones with damaged hoofs, our progress has been good, and after four hours continuous travelling we are nearing Tafila. The odd patch of snow remains where the sun has been unable to reach, and the camels' reaction to it is amusing, particularly when they are required to cross a trickle of melting snow. Without exception they shy away.

Patiently we encourage them to step over the rivulets of water, but they stubbornly refuse and back away with their front hooves searching for a dry footing. Eventually we use our sticks hard on their behinds and with this painful insistence they almost jump across - indeed Barmey hops like a kangaroo and we are amazed by the length of his leap, as the water flow is barely 6 inches across.

Gratefully I pick up some hard snow and rub it into the sores from the rash on the tops of my hands, and for a short while the cold does stop the itching.

As the caravan descends the rocky hillside, I look at the buildings far below and recall that four years ago my view had been from the hill to the north. Then, from its highest point, I had gazed into the red fireball of the setting sun, taken a photograph, studied the tourist map in the car, and decided to drive further south along the King's Highway towards Aqaba.

The guidebook had mentioned little about Tafila, and I was unaware of Lawrence's connection with the place at that time. Nevertheless I remember the sunset as the most dramatic I had witnessed during my travels in the Middle East, and I carry a vivid impression of my first sight of a camel an hour beforehand. As I eagerly photographed it, I never thought that I would one day spend a month riding across the desert on such an animal.

It was for Lawrence's part in the battle of Tafila on 25 January, 1918, that he was awarded the Distinguished Service Order. Lawrence later declined to accept his decorations during a private investiture with King George V - he was supposed to have received the Companion of the Bath and the Distinguished Service Order. Lawrence felt His Majesty's government had not honoured their promises to the Arabs which he had given in his own name. The basis for the decoration was upon his own report of events to General Allenby's headquarters. Later Lawrence was to write of this, 'We should have more bright breasts in the Army if each man was able without witnesses, to write out his own despatch.' The defence of Tafila against three battalions of Turkish infantry was the only regular set-piece battle Lawrence was involved in during the war. The defending force of 300 men under the command of Zeid eventually won the battle and killed 400 Turks with 250 men taken prisoner. Lawrence attributed the victory to the tactical advice he gave the Arabs.

I hold Hashan in a position which gives me advantageous command of the terrain around Tafila. But as I read Lawrence's detailed description of the battle's course I find difficulty in relating his account to the ground. We had hoped to conduct a battlefield tour, and I remark to James how I wish Lawrence had included some maps of his actions in *Seven Pillars*.

When finally we reach the town, our arrival causes quite a stir. We lead our camels along the road up the hill to its centre, and I have to shorten Hashan's rein to prevent him bolting each time a vehicle passes. Crowds of school children follow us in procession up the street, jabbering excitedly and practising on us some of the few English words they know. Their 'Hey Mister!' becomes extremely tiresome after a short while. We couch and unload the camels on an area of waste land off the main street. A large crowd assembles around each of us, scrutinising our every move and then giggling. Some remain quiet and smiling, others are more bold and ask an endless number of questions. As I sit on my saddle bags attempting to plot the route we must take to Shaubak, it amuses me to think that near El Mudawwarah an old vehicle track in the sand had made me feel cheated - now I am resigned to contact with modern Jordan and have little choice but to accept the diesel fumes, throngs of staring people, and the blaring horns of arrogant Arab drivers as they hurtle by. I look up as James returns from a shop with a large bag of Mars bars and I recoil immediately.

To my mind we should still be in the middle of nowhere, maintaining the strain and rigours of our journey without supplies such as these. It is the one subject on which we differ. Although James shares similar sentiments, he also accepts the reality of our situation and sees little point in pretending otherwise - if there is a shop that will provide his body with nourishment, he will use it.

As if to remind me I am no more than a tourist in disguise, a bus bound for Petra stops on the road near our caravan and dozens of pale faces and cameras peer at us through the tinted, curtained windows, eagerly drinking up this vision of authenticity. I feel like an animal in an open zoo. Perhaps the only compensation is that they will never know who we really are. By dusk we have covered a good distance for one day, and are extremely tired, but my worry is whether we will now have sufficient time to reach Aqaba via Wadi Rumm, a route through the hills which would be a fitting end to the journey. The maximum distance we will be able to claim if Aqaba is reached is 750 miles - a far cry from the 1,000-mile expedition I had planned. Over and above the camels and the Bedouin which have hindered our aim, there is now a fresh restriction. At Tafila police post I rang the Embassy to update them on the schedule, and Colonel Whitten informed me Keith Graves of the BBC would film us at Petra. It will mean a further day's delay, precious hours we can barely afford.

8 March

Our route is through Rashadiya to the Crusader Castle at Shaubak. Lawrence covered the same ground on 11 February, 1918, on his she-camel Wodheiha, and on that occasion he rode from Shaubak to meet with the Arab commander Zeid at Tafila. He delivered gold for the payment of his men and further instructions for the winter campaign. His journey had in fact originally begun at Feisal's camp at Guweira three days earlier. With £30,000 in gold coins distributed amongst fourteen men, Lawrence and his escort set off to pay the units of the Arab army, beleaguered in the hills, in the grip of a harsh winter, and defending their gains from the Turks to the north. 'As we set foot on the ascent, Serz looked up and said, "The mountain wears his skull cap." There was a white dome of snow on every crest; and the Ateiba pushed quickly and curiously up the pass to feel this new wonder with their hands. The camels, too, were ignorant, and stretched their slow necks down to sniff the whiteness twice or thrice in tired inquiry.'

Ten miles short of Shaubak the party had split. The snow and cold winter so badly affected the Bedouin that they refused to continue further and sought shelter in a Howeitat camp. Carrying only £6,000 of the £30,000, Lawrence left them to continue to Tafila on his own. He was barefooted. 'The white ice crackled desolately under my naked feet.' Once his camel fell down a hillside into a snow drift and refused to move further.'So I carved her a beautiful little road, a foot wide, three deep, and eighteen paces long, using my bare feet and hands as tools. The snow was so frozen on the surface that it took all my weight, first to break it down, and then to scoop it out. The crust was sharp, and cut my wrists and ankles till they bled freely, and the roadside became lined with pink crystals, looking pale, very pale, water-melon flesh.'

In Lawrence's time the road he followed between Shaubak and Tafila was a Roman one 'with its groups of fallen milestones, inscribed by famous emperors.' Today the only accessible route is via the King's Highway, which twists and winds through the hills. I console myself with its splendid panorama towards the Dead Sea and distant hills of Judaea. The route may be modern but is nonetheless an arduous one and I cannot but admire Lawrence's stamina in such conditions, though wonder at the virtue of bare feet.

We reach the small police fort of Rashadiya before noon and we are invited to eat. However, I notice Mohammed carrying our supplies into the fort and when he brings in more than enough to feed the six of us, I realise that we are to feed a fair number of the police too - in one meal we are down on two days of rations. I can say nothing as it will only cause offence and upset our own Bedouin.

Leaving Rashadiya we descend the hill to the plain. The Wadi Arabah and Dead Sea to our right are nearly indiscernible in the haze of the afternoon sun. It is hot and the lice torment us. We pass through a small shanty village, heading once more across the desert with 12 miles left before Shaubak. I am content with our progress and confident that nightfall will see us sleeping in the Crusader Castle where Lawrence rested on 10 February, 1918. Suddenly there is a shout from behind. I turn to see an Arab running down the slope towards us from the outskirts of the village. We ignore him and continue to walk our camels, heading for an animal trail that leads through a distant wadi, but the shouting persists and I look to see who else he might be calling - of course it can only be ourselves.

The man is joined by another and together they approach, seemingly very irate about something. I assume we must have caused offence by passing through the village without accepting their hospitality, and I do not relish the prospect of a long session around a camp fire drinking tea and swapping stories. But when they arrive, breathless, they begin haranguing Mohammed and Hamed in a manner which is anything but friendly. Mohammed tells me they wish to see our passes, but I produce Brigadier Shobaky's letter of safe conduct. To my surprise they dismiss that and demand to see our cameras, all the time glancing around as if expecting one of us to suddenly try and escape.

Now quite baffled, I ask Mohammed to explain, which prompts a long discourse with the most officious of the two. After much translation it becomes clear that they are arresting us as spies. I am dumbfounded. When I ask what we have been spying on they become secretive, eventually mentioning the radar station on the hill about 3 miles the other side of the village.

Since they are unarmed it does cross my mind to ignore them and continue our journey, but Mohammed is already couching and unloading his camel. Taking me aside from what has become a small crowd, he warns that we must do as the man says, and that Brigadier Shobaky will surely solve things eventually. I agree, realising that to behave like an indignant British officer in a foreign land is unlikely to help, and that in any case the last person I resemble is a British officer, with my dirty and pock-marked thobe, filthy kaffiyah, sunburnt face, beard, and camel-hobbling rope tied around my waist in the fashion of the poorer Bedouin.

Our cameras are collected along with our passes while another of our captors excites a growing crowd of Arabs with tales of sinister English spies about to jeopardise the safety of their land. Those in the crowd eye us intently, their heads turning back and forth to the man who is obviously recounting his brave part in it all.

Only now does it dawn on me just how close we are to the Israeli border. I barely remember passing the radar hill but do recall taking some photographs of the Wadi Arabah from the area of the village... Without further ado Mohammed and I are frog-marched away. When we reach a nearby road, a passing minibus is flagged down. Feeling like prisoners we are hustled aboard and our captor, whom I now discover is a Jordanian army officer, gives rapid instructions to the somewhat bewildered driver. Mohammed sits silent and impassive as the officer excitedly repeats the story to everyone in the vehicle. I feel a total alien. We drive for a few miles before I realise we are heading for the radar station. We are dropped at the gate by the sentry post, and our captor confidently shows his own pass to the armed guards, and explains about Mohammed and myself. We are escorted inside the wire compound which is surrounded by tanks, dugouts, and anti-aircraft positions. I cannot help but see the amusing side of the episode. Here we are, the so-called spies, inside the secret installation we are supposed to have spied on. I look around, admiring its strategic position in relation to Israel. Meanwhile the Jordanian officer is rushing everywhere intent only on finding the highest authority at the base - the guards are surprisingly bored by it all and leave us alone.

After half an hour he returns accompanied by a Jordanian airforce officer. Immediately I notice a difference in attitude. Apologetically he tells us how embarrassed they are, that our identity has been verified, and that we are free to leave. The airforce officer commands the base and speaks some English - he also attended a military course in England. He offers to drive us back in his own car, and as we go along he talks about the base as if I had a right to know every detail. Mohammed resumes his smiling confidence, and our ex-captor sits quietly beside me. When finally we are back with the others, the officer duly explains our innocence to the crowd. Applauding loudly and shaking our hands vigorously, they carry away their hero of the day with much merriment, teasing and jubilation, but not before he has offered to share a mensaff with us. I decline - the episode has already cost us two hours.

9 March

Shaubak is an insignificant town and the Crusader Castle, where Lawrence stayed 67 years ago, is a ruin - only a bare shell remains, the walls crumbled by time and earthquakes (the last being in the 1920s). At 10 am we pause on some high ground overlooking the castle near a few ramshackle buildings. We decide to eat our main meal of the day here before crossing the hills to Petra, a route which will take us far away from any roads. Chris is in a sour mood. He had to retrace the morning's travels for a mile in order to retrieve a blanket that somehow had fallen from his camel. He mutters that in future he will not listen to Mohammed's advice on loading camels, but do it his own way.

An old man climbs the high ground to our front and finally comes to squat by our fire. It is a Bedouin custom that anyone may share food and will be treated as a friend. The old man says little but drinks our tea and eats some bread. He wears a pair of blue pyjamas with an old army sweater on top and a head-cloth - not the most conventional garb we have seen. Mohammed tells him of our journey and the man exclaims in admiration at the mention of the names of Lawrence and Auda, and asks if we know Glubb Pasha. Then he lifts his sweater, proudly revealing the ugly scars of a bullet wound through his stomach, a memento of his service with the Arab Legion. Little of what he says makes any sense, and even Mohammed is happy to allow him to ramble. Eventually he is silent and simply sits with us, as though he has been a member of our party since Wadi Rumm.

A pity; he is so old I had hoped to learn something from him - a shared reminiscence, perhaps a story of someone who knew Lawrence.

The scenery in the afternoon as we ride south-west to Petra is spectacular, and not dissimilar to the brown foothills of lower Nepal through which I had trekked more than ten years ago. A multitude of deep wadis cross our way which drain into the Wadi Arabah, and at times it is hard work encouraging the camels to further endeavours. It is obvious they are very worn by the 600 miles they have already walked. By modern standards it is a journey they are unused to, and the pressure put on them in these last weeks has been intense. They will probably never leave the rough vicinity of Rumm again for the rest of their lives.

Chris has carved a flute from a piece of wood he found several days ago in a ruined Turkish building on the Hejaz railway. Now he ambles along at the rear happily trying to make a noise that sounds musical. Our Bedouin find it humorous and they nickname him 'Saliman' - a name we presume is similar to the Pied Piper.

The horizon is broken by the far-off grey mountains that merge almost transparently into each other in the sunset. Once more it seems we are in a world apart, and a measure of inner content-

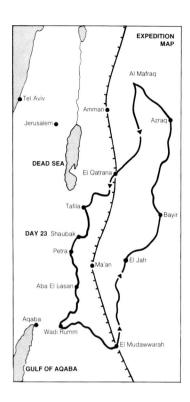

ment returns for the first time since Tafila. Our caravan looks utterly authentic in this almost Biblical setting. We could so easily pass for pilgrims or traders along the spice route to Petra in Jesus' time - that is if one ignores the distant twinkling lights of Israeli settlements to the west.

A small boy trots beside me while holding the slack from Hashan's rein. He had appeared from nowhere and attached himself to us a few miles out of Shaubak. Mohammed gave him a little food and now he goes from one person to the other helping them with their camels. He seems a strange, dim-witted boy - barefooted, extremely dirty and wearing very worn clothes. I feel sorry for this homeless stranger, yet at the same time I do not want an addition to the expedition.

In characteristic form, Mark says that by accompanying us the boy is depriving a village of an idiot. We laugh cruelly and ignorantly.

Eventually I have to tell Mohammed that the boy must go. I realise that this is offensive to him - Arab tradition being to take in a stranger and feed him - but we already have six mouths to feed and there is not going to be a seventh. Mohammed explains the state of affairs to the boy, but he explained it like a father to a son and couldn't say 'Go.'

In the twilight we follow a goat-track downhill towards a small glow of light. Mohammed says it is the village of Hauf, approximately 4 miles north-east of Petra, and soon I can smell woodsmoke and hear goat-bells.

The village turns out to be no more than half-a-dozen old mud and stone-walled houses of the traditional Middle Eastern kind: flat-roofed, single-storied, and with one door and one window. The houses nestle into the rock-face leaving an open flat area to their front, and it is on this that we couch the camels in a circle. It is quite dark but there is a beautiful sky against which are silhouetted the nearby hills. Sounds of bleating goats, the odd metallic bang, the cry of a baby and some indiscernible Arab talk are suspended in the still, cold night-air. There are no electric lights, and the yellow firelight from inside the buildings is inviting and homely. There is a full moon and its gentle pearly radiance seems to sanctify the scene with its pearly radiance. Once more I feel we could be in Biblical times as we sit together patiently waiting for the traditional hospitality. Mohammed tells me it is the custom for travellers to camp a little distance from a village or tent and wait for the owners to respond by offering food and drink. Sure enough, after ten minutes, a man joins our circle and smokes a cigarette with us. He leaves and returns with a boy carrying wood for our fire, a kettle of water and some tea. Eagerly we await the food, expecting bowls of steaming hot goat-meat and bread or rice. None comes.

Instead Mark prepares a quantity of bread, some onions, olives and a couple of tins of bully beef that we had bought in Tafila.

Huddled together about the fire, blankets stretched over our exposed backs between two or three people, we sit drinking tea and eating bread. Eventually we are joined by more than half-a-dozen shepherds and they enjoy our food too. The last of the Tafila rations are finished. I accept it as the proper thing.

Conversation flows, tea cups are refilled, and our sponsor's supplies of Rothmans cigarettes are handed round. Many interesting faces are reflected in the firelight. Later, as I lie in the warmth of my sleeping bag, I observe the silhouette of Hashan by moonlight. Despite recent bad experiences with him (my 'Dash with Hash', as Chris describes it, has unfortunately become a daily occurrence and source of great amusement) I remain fascinated by these extraordinary animals. He lies, neck extended, repeatedly chewing and regurgitating his earlier meal. Occasionally he stops, leans his head to one side or other and listens alert to the slightest sound. Then he returns to gaze directly ahead into the night, head uplifted, and carries on the slow continuous motion of chewing. I wonder if he ever lets his guard drop and lies down to sleep.

10 March

As dawn breaks I watch the people of the village in their morning routine. It is the women who appear first, shepherding the flocks of sheep towards their grazing. The sight is tranquil, and I absorb its detail and colour. The others remain fast asleep, sealed in their one-man shelters, whose taut fabrics are covered in frost.

The camels are couched in a circle closely about our sleeping area, and I have been continually amazed that no accidents have occurred - for despite Hamad hobbling their legs there is always one who succeeds in shifting about. Even as I lie there Barmey moves towards Chris' bivvy bag , brushes past it and sniffs the ground in search of food. Chris is woken by these noises and quickly unzips the hood, pokes his head out of the opening and curses the camel, throwing stones to shoo him away. Unfortunately, however, this takes him closer to Mark.

'Mark, are you awake?' I call also aiming rocks at Barmey.

'Yeah,' comes the muffled and sleepy response.

'There's a camel about to sit on you,' I say affecting a casual tone.

'Where, where, where?' he asks urgently. There is a great deal of sudden movement inside his bivvy bag.

'To your left if you're face down.'

'How near? I'm trying to get out of my sleeping bag but the zip's stuck,' he replies genuinely fearing for his safety.

'Oh, about a foot away.'

Finally Mark's frantic struggles meet with success. The incident, an amusing one, is nonetheless a serious reminder of our constant vulnerability in the desert.

Chapter Nine

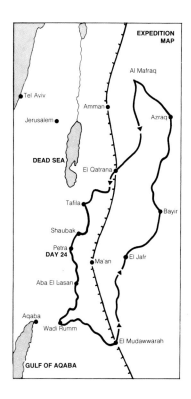

EXPEDITION MAP

Al Mafraq
Tel Aviv
Amman
Jerusalem
Azraq
DEAD SEA
El Qatrana
Tafila
Bayir
Shaubak
Petra
DAY 24
Ma'an
El Jafr
Aba El Lasan
Aqaba
Wadi Rumm
El Mudawwarah
GULF OF AQABA

'The capital of the Nabataen is the so-called Petra, for it lies on ground in general even and level but guarded all around by rock, outside precipitous and abrupt but inside having abundant springs for drawing water and for gardening.'

Thus did the classical writer, Strabo, describe this amazing city. Archaeologists have identified sherds of Greek vases of around 300 BC that show there were at least the beginnings of a town at that time. Further artifacts reveal that during the third and second centuries BC, Petra was gradually built up into a rich centre for the caravan trade from Arabia. Later it was captured by the Romans who re-designed it on the regular Roman model with a main street of columns and buildings either side. The site of the city was lost to the Western world from the time of the Crusades, around AD 1200, until it was rediscovered by an Anglo-Swiss explorer in 1812. But the uniqueness of Petra lies not in its history but in the surviving rock-cut dwellings of the Nabataeans, their tombs carved out of the rugged sandstone peaks which are white, brown and red in colour, and in the facades of buildings cut into the rock and adorned with columns and statues.

The tricky descent from Hauf along the narrow pathways in the hills has taken one and a half hours. It is 8.30 am. From where we stand with our camels at the end of a dried-up water course which leads to Petra, the ancient city is concealed among the smooth-topped limestone mountains. We are surrounded by colourful groups of Arabs standing or squatting together with their horses and ponies tethered nearby. There is much shouting and joking among the different parties, and as I watch it all I think how similar a group of Arab army horsemen would have looked in Lawrence's day. Ponies gallop past, their hooves clattering on the stones, and the riders shout greetings to friends with great bravado.

The Arabs are waiting to hire their ponies to the tourists and offer themselves as guides - the alternative is a mile walk along a winding torrent before the remote city is reached. The Syk, as this is called, is its only entrance and ensures the Arabs a monopoly on tourist transport, which they guard jealously, eyeing us with a degree of suspicion when they see our caravan in case we plan to take any trade from them. Our camels are the only ones to be seen.

Our main concern, however, is that there is no sign of the expected BBC film crew. Already the Ambassador had unfortunately disallowed a story in the Jordanian press, presumably in order to play down past 'Imperial' connections with the country, so I was keen for any publicity to reciprocate the generosity of our sponsors, and surely a more magnificent backdrop than Petra could not be found.

But if we imagined entering this historic place, riding triumphantly towards a BBC camera crew, people at home watching the 'Lawrence of Arabia Expedition' on their television screens, we were to be disappointed. We were met by no-one.

Mohammed tells me it will be wrong to take the camels into Petra since it will upset the pony owners. But we have not ridden all this way to be denied so unique an opportunity, and I head for the tourist office to obtain the necessary permission to stay the night.

My arrival at the office, which is staffed by immaculately dressed Jordanians, causes some consternation. I am shown a large black leather chair and immediately become aware of how foul I smell. The still air in the warm room seems to increase the activity of the lice and self-consciously I scratch away at the invisible vermin. After a good deal of bargaining and explaining, my requests are granted. The one man who speaks English tells me that it is of course a privilege, rarely allowed. Also he knows nothing of any film crew in Petra.

I ring the Embassy and speak to Colonel Whitten who is surprised to hear we have reached Petra so quickly. He says he hopes to visit us the following morning and that Keith Graves will not be coming after all - the recent Iranian bombing of Baghdad is a major news item and his team have been diverted there.

The disappointment at the lack of publicity (the promise of which had been an important source of morale to us) fades as we ride majestically past the Arabs who wait patiently for the first influx of tourist coaches. Despite a visit four years ago the magic of the moment is not lost to me now. There is virtual silence as the rocks on either side close in and we ride along the narrow Syk, the walls of which are hundreds of feet high. Here it is cool, the only light coming from the small opening to the sky far above; sometimes the rock almost meets overhead. The twisting passage is along a large fissure in the rock formation, and through this opening (only 6 feet wide in places) we guide our camels. Hashan abruptly shies away from the rock on a couple of occasions, no doubt having never before been in such a confined area.

James as he arrives in the city. '"Brilliant Petra," Lawrence called it...but there is something spellbinding about the place.'

Some birds are calling high above us and I catch the odd glimpse of them as they flit between the rock ledges and the little greenery that clings to the steep sides. My palms sweat in anticipation of rounding the final bend where we will be met by the first sight of the Treasury building, richly carved into the red sandstone, a blaze of colour after the dark shadows of the Syk. The next moment it is there in the sunlight and the others gasp in astonishment at the unexpected and imposing sight. It is as rose red as I

'My palms sweat in anticipation of rounding the final bend where we will be met by the first sight of the Treasury building, richly carved into the red sandstone, a blaze of colour after the dark shadows of the Syk. The next moment it is there...the others gasp in astonishment.'

remember and I derive no less pleasure from this second encounter.

Like all the large monuments the Treasury is carved from the rock. The lines of the columns and tiers of the facade seem to be perfectly intact. At the top a large urn has been badly battered by rifle fire. Folk lore has it that it contains a vast fortune of gold and many people have sought to break it - hence the building's name, El Khaznah (the Treasury). It glows in the sun as though itself radiating light, and the effect is enhanced by the dark green, and delicate pink flowers of the oleander bushes in the foreground.

Mohammed and Hamad appear unmoved, even though they have never been in Petra before. I find this strange considering how famous it is; for most tourists it is a priority visit. But of course the concept of sight-seeing is utterly unintelligible to the Bedouin. (Our camel handlers had expressed no interest in the castle at Azraq, earlier.)

I suppose that, as desert tribesmen, the lives of Mohammed and Hamad revolve entirely around their families and their harsh existence, leaving no room for broader cultural interests. Theirs do not appear to be minds sensitive to such as Petra's beauty. Yet it was Lawrence who noted how 'even the unsentimental Howeitat had told me it was lovely' when talking of Wadi Rumm on his first journey there.

The magnificence of this ancient place unfurls as we ride past the Nabataean caves, the Roman amphitheatre of a later period, past the Palace Tomb, the tomb of the Roman soldier carved into the steep rock face whose strata are the colours of the rainbow, through the paved Roman Colonnade, and we revel in it. Dismounting near the Nabataean temple in an open place by the Roman archway, we sit for some while in the morning light and admire this wonder of civilisation about us. It is certainly the finest camping place we have found! But there is something spellbinding about Petra - it is difficult not to be enchanted by such colour and so many monuments.

As Petra is our first proper break since Azraq I sleep for while and then begin updating the expedition diary and photolog. It is also a welcome opportunity to read from *Seven Pillars of Wisdom*, this time with the advantage of having been nearly a month in the desert following the same journeys. 'Brilliant Petra' is Lawrence's single entry of where we are, and his omission of further detail surprises me since his route took him through Wadi Musa* one mile from Petra. He must have visited the city, especially since he was such a keen archaeologist and ardent classicist. By contrast 'Rum the magnificent' and 'Azraq the remote' prompted some of his most inspired prose, such was their impact upon him.

Crowds of tourists come and go throughout the day. Hordes of Japanese with cameras, fat women on little ponies being charmed by their Bedouin guides, excitable groups of French and the less gregarious English who quietly follow their own guide books. We sit near the Roman Colonnade and watch with amusement, relishing our disguises.

Our 'privileged position' determines the manner with which we are treated by the local people, who mainly dwell with their families in caves, the mouths of which are blocked by walls with only small doorways and windows. They live virtually as custodians to the city. One man, who owns the Palace Tomb, its two entrances leading to chambers carefully shaped into large square rooms, invites our party to be his guests for a mensaff and to spend the night. We gratefully accept his hospitality.

By dusk the last tourists are gone and Petra returns to silence. The shadows of the rock intensify and the caves are lit by fires as their inhabitants settle for the night. Inside our host's cave we lie on cushions and rugs round a fire of thick timbers. The floor is sandy and cleanly swept. The chamber has been precisely cut, the ancient tool marks of the work still visible, and the entrance is some height above the ground so we can look out and down on part of Petra. Directly opposite, and at the foot of the far hills, is the Nabataean temple, with the Roman Colonnade leading towards it along the wadi bottom.

We eat chicken mensaff served on a huge circular dish as we squat on the floor. The thin strips of bread are rolled up and

---

*Literally translated this is the Wadi of Moses. It is the legendary place where Moses struck the rock from which came water. Today a stream flows down the hill near the village into Petra and it remains the only supply of water.

'Couching the camels at Petra - our first proper break since Azraq, so I sleep for a while and then begin updating the expedition diary and photo log. It is also a welcome opportunity to read from Seven Pillars of Wisdom.*'*

dipped into the delicious juice. We are ravenous and could easily devour the food in one sitting, but for Mohammed motioning us away when we had finished. Reluctantly we move aside to allow the family to have the second sitting which will be taken to the women and children in the other cave. One by one we hold out our hands to allow a small boy to pour water over them. We then return to our places by the fire and another boy serves coffee in small china cups without handles. It has a bitter but distinctive taste which is refreshing. Finally the glasses are filled with sweet tea and this completes the evening's feasting. Now the stories will begin and the tea and coffee will continue to circulate until it is time to sleep.

I lie contentedly smoking my pipe and listen to the animated conversation between four Bedu; their huge shadows cast by the fire dance against the rock in time with the flames. Through the entrance to the cave is an almost azure-coloured sky, full of bright stars, and the sigh of the wind on the rock face blends with the sound of singing from far away. It is a beautiful setting in which I feel completely at peace, wanting never to leave and return to the daily bustle of life in the Western world.

The old man who is our host's father produces something similar to a banjo. He tells us it is a 'rababa' which is an ancient Bedouin

instrument and made by stretching goatskin tightly over a hollow wood frame. A single string of plaited horse hair extends from the cleft over a bridge to the bottom of the instrument. The man proudly announces that he made it, and begins to pluck the taut string and sing in a slow, sustained monotone. It is surprisingly pleasant and, encouraged by our approval, he sings several more songs.

'The local people mainly dwell with their families in caves, the mouths of which are blocked by walls with only small doorways and windows. They live virtually as custodians to the city.'

The rababa is then passed to his son, and songs of the Howeitat in love and war echo through the cave and away into the night. The instrument is next passed around the fire to Mohammed who shyly accepts it. I begin to wonder if he is embarrassed to compare his ability with the others. But quickly I realise my mistake. As he plays, he looks at me with an enquiring expression and sings beautifully. I am fascinated by the assuredness of his playing, the manner with which his fingers glide up and down the string. It is another side of this extraordinary man, and as the last notes die away we are silent and profoundly moved. Laughing now, he knows he has proved himself a maestro before mere amateurs, and hands the instrument to Hamad. But the rough tone of Hamad's simple playing lacks Mohammed's feeling and breaks the spell completely.

Suddenly the dark outlines of two men, partially obscured by smoke from the fire, appear at the entrance.

'Salaam alaykum,'(Peace be upon you,) greets one of them, and we rise to return the salutation.

'Alaykum assalaam.' (And upon you be peace.) They enter and I see that they are both Europeans and one carries what can only be a picnic box. As they settle with the Bedouin around the fire I assume they must be old friends, and somehow I resent them spoiling our evening.

'Which of you is Captain Blackmore?' one of them asks in a cultured English voice. The light is so bad we can barely identify the speaker. When I reply, the man introduces himself as Bill Trustram-Eve, the manager of the nearby Petra Hotel. The second man, who is now clearly visible, is wearing a battered safari suit, and introduces himself in a strong American accent as Jefferson Price III. He is the Middle East correspondent for the Baltimore Sun and, hearing of our journey, has travelled from Jerusalem to write an article.

With this, Bill announces he has brought champagne to toast our accomplishment, and promptly produces from the box some glasses and two dark green bottles sparkling with cold droplets of water. The entire episode strikes me as utterly bizarre yet I cannot openly resent their arrival: certainly if our experiences are to be intruded upon by everything we have tried to leave behind, then it may as well be done with style. Moreover, following our disappointment at the cancellation of the Keith Graves interview, we can now count on Jefferson promoting a story of the expedition. Both men are very excited by our venture, and Jefferson is surprised no other paper has followed the story. He jokes that it took the American Lowell Thomas to find Lawrence* and it has taken another American to find the 1985 Lawrence of Arabia Expedition. We chuckle over this extraordinary situation, sitting surrounded by Bedouins in a Nebataean cave in Petra, drinking the champagne. It is another reminder of how two separate worlds constantly collide - one moment talking Arabic, listening to the 'rababa' and drinking tea, the next talking English to an American correspondent and drinking a hotel's best champagne lately from the freezer. It is more extraordinary still when Bill informs us that some of his family before him have been in The Royal Green Jackets.

It is late and Jefferson is tired after his long journey. The champagne is finished, and they stand to leave having arranged to meet us in the morning for the interview and photo session. Once they have departed I realise our evening with the Bedouin had ended with the interruption. Now, it is as though a line has been drawn between us. In particular Mohammed appears to

*Lowell Thomas has been credited with being responsible for the international reputation and ensuing legend of Lawrence. His illustrated lecture tours in the 1920s became instant sell-outs all over the world.

Lawrence sitting next to Lowell Thomas, the American journalist who was largely responsible for the birth of the Lawrence legend through his articles, lectures and 'travelogues'. Opinions vary as to much Lawrence resented this stardom. As Bernard Shaw wrote of Lawrence - 'When he was in the middle of the stage, with ten limelights blazing on him, everybody pointed to him and said: "See! He is hiding. He hates publicity."'

Lawrence shadow boxed with his own image, at times implying how little conscious control he had over his role in the desert wars: 'I had one craving all my life - for the power of expression in some imaginative form - but had been too diffuse ever to acquire a technique. At last accident, with perverted humour, in casting me as a man of action had given me place in the Arab Revolt, a theme ready and epic to a direct eye and hand, thus offering me an outlet in literature, the technique-less art.' Seven Pillars of Wisdom

resent each occasion that we have unthinkingly lapsed into our Western habits - on this occasion it was the champagne that caused offence, as well as the way the Bedouin were excluded from the conversation. They had sat listening to us and I had feared they might feel we were talking about them.

We were exposed. Englishmen merely dressed up in Bedouin clothing. All a pretence.

Having ensured we have sufficient cushions, our Howeitat host leaves to sleep with his family in the other cave. In the darkness, except for the red embers of the fire, I listen to the barking of dogs far away...echoing through the wadi. It is a haunting noise,

'My heaven might have been a lovely, soft arm-chair, a book-rest, and the complete poets, set in Caslon, printed on tough paper.' Seven Pillars of Wisdom

Mohammed with the camels, couched in the process of being fed at the original Petra camping site.

'Outside the Treasury we line our camels up in the small square facing the Syk through which ponies and tourists enter Petra at a steady rate... I bring out the regimental flag.'

almost a moan, carried upon the wind like the sighs of the restless dead of Petra. The centuries can be felt in the atmosphere and I think of the Nabataeans and the Romans in the time of Christ, who must also have lain awake in this cave, just listening.

11 March

'I heard one of those Arabs speaking English,' says an elderly American woman to her companion.

'Yes, and some of them have blue eyes too,' the other woman replies from behind her camera as she photographs us riding past.

Prime tourist time is mid-morning before the heat becomes unbearable and the light is still gentle enough to bring out the best colours of the rock. From our lofty perches we ride with ease and skill, even enjoying the attention while roaming through the main area of the city. Jefferson Price runs ahead taking photographs, and we rearrange our head-cloths and strike poses to look as dashing as possible. Outside the Treasury we line the camels up in the small square facing the Syk through which ponies and tourists enter Petra at a steady rate.

After pictures have been taken from several angles I bring out the regimental flag from my saddle bag. James holds the other side as we proudly stretch it between us, while at the same time struggling hard to control our camels. It is the expedition's third unfurling of the flag and our camel handlers are quite used to the

Mohammed and Hamad with another Arab in Petra.

'Mohammed talked to Druze in Azraq and they were completely different. Mohammed was lost...they spoke the same language, were in the same country and so all Jordanians, but they weren't Howeitat ...and we're talking about a distance of 300 miles...different upbringing, different traditions. But when Mohammed met other Howeitat at Petra he could relate to them.'

pageantry now. At the end of the Syk facing the Treasury and ourselves stand two large groups of French tourists complete with guides. They point at us, take photographs and obviously enjoy the sight of such an Arabian scene. Jefferson comes across and stands beneath me sweating profusely, looking every inch the journalist with all his cameras and lenses.

'Don't you think you should put that flag away?' he says. All those Frogs over there want to know why Waterloo, Calais and Somme are written over the badge.'

He refers to the battle honours and I relish another opportunity to taunt tourists. It seems particularly appropriate since Lawrence loathed the French, and did everything in his power to prevent French territorial gains in the Middle East during and after the war.

The press session complete, we return to the original camping site. It begins to cloud over and as the novelty of Petra is waning I decide to push on once more.

'James' camel became totally uncontrollable during the morning, and now we watch with fascination as our handlers remedy this.

James' camel became totally uncontrollable during the morning, and now we watch with fascination as our handlers remedy this. Struggling with uncertainty and fear the animal is turned on its side, legs tied securely together, and sat on by some assisting Bedu. Mohammed draws his curved dagger and while Hamad pulls hard on the camel's nostrils, the blade is driven sharply into the one remaining untorn one. Mohammed turns the knife like a skewer until there is an adequate hole - the screams of the camel attract a small crowd of spectators.

Next Mohammed plucks large handfuls of hair from the animal's tail, rolls them between the flat of his hands and fashions a length of rope. One end is fed through the hole in the nostril, and when it becomes stuck the sharp blade is used to prod it through. The ends are tied together to form a ring, and to this is knotted a

'We sit awkwardly handling knives and forks and eating off plates for the first time since Aqaba, and begin to feel guilty about our swaggering claims of hardship.'

Lawrence wrote of the difficulty of shedding his previous way of life in the desert, and of the proximity of madness '...as I believe it would be near the man who could see things through the veils at once of two customs, two educations, two environments.' Seven Pillars of Wisdom

thin piece of rope that will reach the rider. This crude technique looks extremely painful and is the second example of how Bedouin can treat camels that we have seen. When the animal is finally released it kicks its feet dangerously, stands up and begins jumping around in a frenzy. Mohammed merely pulls on the nose rope to bring the poor animal to heel. Judging by his expression James intends to use the new rein with a vengeance.

With the arrival of Colonel David Whitten and his wife Rosemary, we are treated by Jefferson to a meal in the outdoor restaurant near the Nabataean temple. As we sit awkwardly handling knives and forks and eating off plates for the first time since Aqaba, we begin to feel guilty about our swaggering claims of hardship. Clearly it would be ridiculous to eat our meagre rations of arbood in these circumstances, but the worst feeling is one of betrayal to the life we share so closely with Mohammed and Hamad. Since it is a conventional 'European' meal we sit at a table observed by them near the camels. The distance between us is apparent. I feel increasingly uncomfortable and wish it had never occurred - it is as though a race and class barrier has descended, and I hate it.

The Bedouin do not understand the machinations of the press or that the story of Lawrence should appeal so much to the Western world. In their eyes he was a greatly respected Englishman who fought in the Arab revolt, but that is all history. Yet to us Lawrence remains an enigmatic legend, surrounded by rumour and controversy, and we have chosen to follow him like ghost hunters. In so doing we have proved ourselves poor and inadequate representatives. Our apparent unrobing in front of Mohammed and Hamad makes it an unhappy day and I wish to leave Petra directly. However there is little to be achieved by this and I have to wait for a dawn start for the final leg through the Abu el Lassan to Rumm.

Our delay in Petra to appease our search for publicity has cost us valuable time in which we could have ridden into Aqaba.

Chapter Ten

12 March

All pretence at a dignified exit from Petra is shattered when Hashan breaks into a wild gallop, and I have no control of him as we pass the Treasury building and head into the Syk. I cling desperately with one hand onto the pommel, while with the other keeping my head-cloth from flying off. I duck to narrowly miss the rock overhangs as we race through the winding passage and out into the sunlight. With head down and neck extended Hashan ignores my attempts to rein him in, seemingly determined to be rid of me once and for all. A few early morning tourists scatter in terror as we round the corners of the wadi and head for the groups of Arabs with their ponies. After my somewhat superior parade through Petra yesterday I feel ridiculous as I gallop past, amid cheers of delight and laughter. It must be the most amusing exit by a European for many years. Hashan's flight frightens the ponies and for a second I fear they will stampede.

As suddenly as he bolted, Hashan comes to a halt. Nonchalantly chewing the tops of a bush he turns his head to regard me with a supercilious expression. Exasperated by his behaviour, and with trembling legs, I jump down to inspect the damage - apparently Hashan is unharmed, one grain sack is missing, and there are a couple of deep cuts on my bare ankles. For this to happen just when I was feeling in control is slightly unnerving. And now, having caught me up, Mohammed is worried about Hashan, and Hamad is annoyed, accusing me of beating the animal which I had not done.

Sitting me down, Mohammed rips off a length of red cloth which he binds around my broken sandal to prevent it from rubbing one of the bleeding areas. His tender fatherly concern in these ministrations is touching. It is Mohammed's way and I gratefully accept his care, not wanting to cause offence by asking Chris for a clean bandage from the medical bag. Somehow his gesture brings us together again and eradicates the shame of yesterday.

We water the camels at a hillside spring in Wadi Musa before continuing our journey towards Aba El Lasan. There, on 2 July, 1917, Lawrence was involved in a battle against a Turkish infantry battalion. Our route retraces a number of his subsequent journeys from Guweira (a headquarters for a while and half way between Rumm and Aba El Lasan) to Tafila and back. These he mapped and described as passing through Wadi Musa, Waheida, El Mureigha and Aba El Lasan. From the now bat-

Leaving Wadi Musa for Aba El Lasan, where Lawrence was involved in a battle against a Turkish infantry battalion.

tered Jordanian Army map with its plastic casing full of grit and sand. I work out our course, noticing with pleasure that it takes us from the road.

The route decided, we begin to ascend a steep hill and the camels labour under their loads, reluctant it seems to move after two days of rest. There is no wind and the valley is very hot and humid. Our Bedouin exchanged sharp words by the spring and now Hamad sulks at the rear. Before I can ask the nature of the issue a noisy argument develops between them - it is another Arab problem I do not understand, and we wait on the incline watching them as their tempers visibly flare. Never before has Hamad appeared so strident, in the past always appearing the quiet one rather subservient to Mohammed. Soon I intervene to bring about a solution. Hamad claims the route is bad and that Mohammed is sick in the head because he is old and arrogant with no consideration for the camels. In reply Mohammed tells me Hamad is an old woman who knows nothing of camels. Three weeks ago the situation would have worried me, but now I have sufficient experience to find their petty rivalry amusing. Mohammed sits down and it is his turn to sulk while Hamad determinedly takes the lead.

'Hamad chief, he go, he chief now,' complains Mohammed with a dismissive wave of his hand. 'Hamad and Mohammed, money same, same - Mohammed no more chief,' he adds with a reproachful look that suggests I have undermined his original status. For the first time I appreciate how, as my confidence has developed, I have left Mohammed out of much of the running of the expedition. In addition, how I have taken him for granted and that he really does look to me for support. Whereas in the early days I felt that the Bedouin were hindering our journey by pursuing their own ideas, I am surprised to realise that in fact they are not as self-assured as I imagined. In understanding their dependence on us now, I become aware of another bond in our

141

relationship that I have overlooked.

Knowing I must restore the balance I order Mohammed to lead and tell him he is a good guide. He continues to sulk and mutters that Hamad is now chief. I insist and he reluctantly agrees. We move on, and tolerantly ignore their squabbling and the occasional shouted insults at each other, muttering to themselves between times. Knowing Hamad has lost face, I tactfully drop to the rear of the caravan and he responds well to my encouragement as diplomatically I play out my role. It is an interesting incident which justifies a remark James made earlier about the Bedouin having the mentality of an English teenager in certain respects whilst, in others, they have a wisdom beyond most educated men.

It is late afternoon when we crest a small rise to enter the shanty village of El Mureigha. The desert begins where the peripheral buildings end, a transition marked by strewn litter and piles of rusting tins. It is unbelievably dirty and depressing after the clean terrain we have crossed. James suggests that it is probably due to the Bedu not understanding what to do with man-made rubbish. Around the goat-hair tents in the desert it is normally spotless, and before the arrival of consumer products there was little that a family threw out which would not organically decay. Despite the Jordanian government policy of bringing tribesmen out of the desert and into villages with pre-fabricated buildings, they retain many of their previous habits. This is evident in the odd tent pitched between the buildings, and it appears that their refuse is thrown outside without a second thought to whether it will or will not disappear. Loose coils of wire become entangled around the legs of our camels, and once again we are confronted with a different desert to that of Lawrence.

'Miranda...Miranda,' says Hamad as we pass a shack with empty crates of this orangeade drink piled outside. We stop on the dusty trail and regard the shop. It would be ridiculous to ignore the chance of a cool drink, yet my initial reaction is to ignore the opportunity. It is certainly true that Lawrence himself made his later journeys across the desert in a Rolls Royce tender, a fact which rather calls into question my own expectation for an existence uncluttered by modern conveniences. Why do I need to see this journey into the desert as an escape? Why am I incapable of facing up to the reality of my own time?

In fact only Coca Cola is served and I watch Hamad greedily drink from the bottle. Mohammed gracefully declines - it is as though he feels as I do, and will not indulge in anything which he considers 'un-Bedouin'. For this I admire him though I am saddened by the changes which will inevitably be forced upon him. His way of life suddenly seems very vulnerable. He squats by his camel with the dignity and humility of the desert nomad - facing him are the town Arabs of a new era who are fascinated to see camels in the dirty streets of El Mureigha.

A car draws up driven by a European. We ignore it.

'Say, are you guys the Green Jackets following Lawrence of Arabia?' the driver calls. He introduces himself as Bill Lyons, a freelance photographer, and we have yet another American on our trail. Bill tells us he has been frustrated in his attempts to photograph HRH Prince Charles and Princess Diana who are staying in Aqaba on a private holiday - apparently the security is so tight that no journalists or photographers are allowed near the sea port. Hearing of our exploits he has driven all day to find us. Five minutes later and we would have disappeared into the desert heading for Aba El Lasan.

I am a little embarrassed to be caught in surroundings so unsym-pathetic to the Lawrence legend. What's more, we have no stories of dysentery, dying camels or experiences at the hands of bri-gands in the desert to relate, only a little hardship and a few lice. Nevertheless, he is eager for some photographs before the light goes, and when he has set himself up at a vantage point, we ride towards him along a disused railway line. After two runs he is still unhappy over the quality of the shots and asks us to do another. Mohammed cannot see the reasoning behind it and refuses. He rides off alone to halt some distance away, shouting to me that we will camp there. I have no intention of doing so but Mohammed is already unloading his camel and laying out his rugs. I am reassured when Hamad does not join him.

When the third run is complete, Bill is satisfied and we ride towards Mohammed before heading south to Aba El Lasan. I feel sorry for him as he sits alone by his couched camel and do not enjoy appearing to usurp his authority. However it is I who must lead and we are tired of Mohammed's repeated tantrums and his attempts to call the tune. I tell him we must continue for one more hour and lead on, fearing all the time we might end up camping in two groups and that it is the end of our friendship. Hamad stops

'Bill Lyons is eager for some photographs and when he has set himself up at a vantage point, we ride towards him along a disused railway line...Mohammed refuses and rides off alone...'

to talk with him before following us, and after a few hundred yards I turn to see Mohammed dejectedly reloading his camel. There is no joy in this victory - it is quite unlike the tentative battles for superiority with the Bedouin en route to El Mudaw-warah.

In less than an hour it is dark and we camp where there is brushwood for a fire. As usual, Hamad tends the camels, while Mark arranges a meal of bread and two tins of bully beef between us. Mohammed says nothing, but wraps the sheepswool jacket around himself and stares intently into the flames. Looking at him I appreciate how fatiguing the journey has been for someone of his age, (indeed, he has twice as many years as nearly all of us). He looks utterly defeated and I am deeply hurt to see him so. Hamad takes no advantage of this - on the contrary he looks after him with the same care he displayed when Mohammed was ill before Qatrana.

13 March

We travel for one hour across rocky terrain before descending into the shallow valley of Aba El Lasan. A rough, pot-holed road runs its length, and opposite the steep incline of a hill are a few randomly spaced buildings.

The camels are unloaded in the open sandy area beside a well, our arrival unremarkable to the occasional Bedu who are resting nearby. In spite of it being 8 am the sun is hot and the early stop is welcome. We are tired and lethargic, a result of the phsical hardship and the mental strain of a month together. I feel irrita-ble towards the others for the first time on the journey, unimpressed by their apparent acceptance of everything, and over-sensitive about the responsibiliity and purpose of the trip which I have taken upon myself. Also thoughts of yesterday's clash with Mohammed remain, and unlike previous arguments the coming of a new day did not relax the tension between us. This personality clash troubles me and I long to be rid of the need to come to terms with the strange ways of the Bedouin. It is a claustrophobic feeling unlike the novelty of earlier discoveries about them, and one which I know is exaggerated by the immi-nence of our journey's end.

Sitting on a saddle bag beside Hashan I look at the strata of limestone outcrops a few hundred yards away, aware that it was against them that the Turkish infantry battalion sought cover from the Bedouin rifle fire on that day in July 1917. At the same time it does not stir my imagination. It was different at Rumm, Mudawwarah, Bayir and Azraq - at those places I could feel the atmosphere of the Arab Revolt and easily picture Lawrence amongst it all. Sadly now my senses seem dulled by familiarity. It is even an effort to read *Seven Pillars of Wisdom* to understand what happened here. I realise how tired I am of the desert and the Bedouin, and in this state of apathy I can appreciate what Lawrence must have felt in his own moments of isolation.

Notwithstanding these feelings I resolve to make the best of our time, and with *Seven Pillars* as our guide to the battlefield we climb the high ground behind the steep limestone outcrop. It is a task we do not take to with any enthusiasm - the valley is still and humid with prickly scrub underfoot. At the highest point our view is a commanding one with the village dominated by the amphitheatre of hills around. The others sit on boulders as I read Lawrence's account and attempt to reconstruct the battle he describes. The Turkish infantry battalion had spent the night of 1 July, 1917, by the roadside spring of Aba El Lassan, the site of today's well. While they were in possession of that pass the road to Aqaba was blocked to the Arab army, and at this stage the capture of the sea port was the key to the campaign. The Bedouin forces therefore surrounded the hills in a wide circle and sniped at the Turks, hoping to force them out into the open.

As Lawrence wrote:

'We ran up and down to supply our lack of numbers by mobility, ever looking over the long ranges of hill for a new spot from which to counter this or that Turkish effort.' The exchanges of rifle fire continued all day and it became so hot that 'the rocks on which we flung ourselves for aim were burning, so that they scorched our breasts and arms, from which later the skin drew off in ragged sheets.'

We survey the shimmering hills, shading our eyes from the March sun. Only now can we imagine the July heat and the Bedouin in their pale robes creeping from rock to rock, exchanging hasty shots with the uniformed Turks below. For a brief moment I am away from Mohammed, my actions are not scrutinized, and I can forget the problems of the present and concentrate on the real purpose of the expedition. As a result, it is easier to recapture the atmosphere and scene of the battle. Mark and Chris even begin to look closely at the ground, perhaps hoping to spot an ejected brass cartridge case fired from a Bedouin rifle.

The crux of the battle was Auda Abu Tayi's reckless charge at the head of 50 horsemen. He had been spurred into action by an insulting remark Lawrence had made earlier about the Howeitat, 'they shoot a lot and hit a little.' To the south-west of the spring 400 camel men waited out of sight of the enemy. Lawrence and Nasir, an Arab leader, were with them when they heard plenty of yelling and firing of shots.

'We kicked our camels furiously to the edge, to see our fifty horsemen coming down the last slope into the main valley like a run-away, at full gallop, shooting from the saddle. As we watched, two or three went down, but the rest thundered forward at marvellous speed, and the Turkish infantry, huddled together under the cliff ready to cut their desperate way out towards

Maan, in the first dusk began to sway in and out, and finally broke before the rush, adding their flight to Auda's charge.'

To our right the ground dips and then rises to a crest below the level of the spring, forming a gentle slope down towards the old Maan road 500 yards away. By piecing together the clues on the terrain and layout of the forces, we estimate the fold in the ground is where Lawrence and Nasir waited. Walking from the bottom of it, we reach the highest point in such a position as to be able to visualize Auda's charge into the main valley from the west. The key to Lawrence's position in the battle comes later when he is involved in a camel charge against the fleeing troops - he says they came over the eastward slope. Since the troops were fleeing down the valley road towards Maan they would be heading east, therefore we feel confident about the location of the 400 cameliers at the next important stage of the battle.

'Nasir screamed at me, "Come on," with his bloody mouth; and we plunged our camels madly over the hill, and down towards the head of the fleeing enemy. The slope was not too steep for a camel-gallop, but steep enough to make their pace terrific, and their course uncontrollable: yet the Arabs were able to extend to right and left and to shoot into the Turkish brown. The Turks had been too bound up in the terror of Auda's furious charge against their rear to notice us as we came over the eastward slope: so we also took them by surprise in the flank; and a charge of ridden camels going nearly thirty miles an hour was irresistible.'

We walk down the slope with a sense of excitement over what must be the 'battlefield'. The copse is to the left, but judging by the severity of the dip in the ground beyond it is more likely the camel charge headed directly for the valley floor and thus a little to the right. I stop and try to picture the sheer scale and noise of 400 camels galloping downhill, their riders brandishing swords and firing their rifles, beserk in their bloodlust for the enemy.

'I had got among the first of them, and was shooting, with a pistol of course, for only an expert could use a rifle from such plunging beasts; when suddenly my camel tripped and went down emptily upon her face, as though pole-axed. I was torn completely from the saddle, sailed grandly through the air for a great distance, and landed with a crash which seemed to drive all the power and feeling out of me' - unconscious for a while, Lawrence then 'sat up and saw the battle over, and our men driving together and cutting down the last remnants of the enemy. My camel's body had lain behind me like a rock and divided the charge into two streams and in the back of its skull was the heavy bullet of the fifth shot I fired.'

Chris takes a photograph of the three of us standing in the area where we assume Lawrence fell. Without a map of the battle it can only be an approximation, and James suggests finding a local Bedouin who might know the facts. Nevertheless we are pleased and, as at the castle in Azraq, stimulated by using *Seven Pillars of*

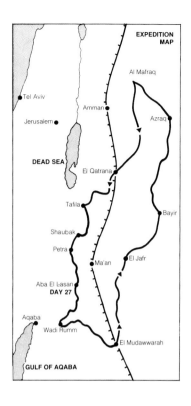

EXPEDITION MAP

Wisdom to help bring a small piece of history alive.

There were 160 prisoners taken, and Lawrence calculated some 'three hundred dead and dying were scattered over the open valleys.' After the battle he met with Auda who 'held up his shattered field-glasses, his pierced pistol-holster, and his leather sword-scabbard cut to ribbons. He had been the target of a volley which had killed his mare under him, but the six bullets through his clothes had left him scathless.'

As we walk back up the valley to the camels I have a clear mental picture of the Turkish dead, the smell of battle, the clouds of dust, roaming camels and Bedouin stripping the bodies of their enemies. Lawrence had been here on this exact spot, yet the bare rock carries no record, no epitaph and only those in search of the past would be aware of it. I reflect on how transient human exploit is; the event may have been critical to those men at that moment - it was their present. But today, though the scenery is the same, there is nothing to honour history - it is no longer even important. Since no evidence remains it may not have happened at all.

It is the decisions of men that have lasting historical implications, rarely the physical actions of the moment. It is a theme I relate to the Middle East in particular. Lawrence's work, the daring exploits of Auda Abu Tayi and his Howeitat, the minor and major actions against the Turks, are insignificant compared with the far-reaching decisions of statesmen. The settlements made at the Peace Conference in Paris in 1919 decided the future of the Middle East, not the little valley at Aba El Lassan.

It is now 10 am, and Mohammed greets our return with something of his old charm, handing us tea to drink before we depart south. The final leg of the journey is soon to begin. Mohammed's attitude relieves me and it appears he has benefited from his short time away from us. He also knows he will soon be home in Wadi Rumm. I finish my reading of *Seven Pillars of Wisdom* with Lawrence's account of walking along the valley where the fighting had taken place. It is one which strikes me as being dramatic and macabre, at the same time presenting him as a chivalrous knight on a medieval battlefield honouring the fallen foe.

'The dead men looked wonderfully beautiful. The night was shining gently down, softening them in new ivory. Turks were white-skinned on their clothed parts, much whiter than the Arabs; and these soldiers had been very young. Close round them lapped the dark wormwood, now heavy with dew, in which the ends of the moon-beams sparkled like sea-spray. The corpses seemed flung so pitifully on the ground, huddled anyhow in low heaps. Surely if straightened they would be comfortable at last. So I put them all in order, one by one, very wearied myself, and longing to be these quiet ones, not of the restless, noisy, aching mob up the valley, quarrelling over the plunder, boasting of their speed and strength to endure God knew how many toils and pains of this sort; with death, whether we won or lost, waiting to end the history.'

Looking now at the width of the valley, and the length along which the dead would have been spread in their flight from the area of the spring, I am fascinated by Lawrence's actions. In the aftermath of the battle, weary and suffering from the effects of the fall, it would be a large undertaking for a man of Lawrence's size. I check my initial scepticism as I analyse his descriptions and compare them to the scene I can picture. Who am I to sit there in 1985 casting opinion on an incident in 1917, I think. In any case my recollections of our journey in one year will be distorted by time, a process which highlights the favourable memories and tends to shadow the less pleasant ones. The full effect is lost with its translation into prose unless writing with Lawrence's intensity of description. Therefore I search no further for the meaning or the real interpretation of his passages. Instead I admire the manner in which he makes this insignificant and magnificent limestone around me come alive with history and splendour.

Chapter Eleven

From Rasr Naqb our caravan descends the hill to the Guweira plain, which is a sudden and dramatic change of scenery. We leave behind the hills we have travelled through since Wadi Hesa, and enter a sandy plain broken only by hillocks. It looks like a sea of pale yellow sandstone hills rising abruptly from the desert, their irregular surfaces eroded in interesting configurations. Delicate wisps of cloud blur the sun and filter the direct sunlight which would otherwise bring out the full colour of the view. Occasional shafts of silvery light penetrate the cloud gaps in the far distance, their diagonal lines parallel to each other giving the impression of some greater power reaching into our world.

At the foot of the plain we wait near tamarisk bushes to allow Chris to catch up. It is warmer than in the hills and the resulting humidity encourages my lice and also makes the rashes on my hands more uncomfortable. Chris appears after ten minutes having taken a different route although the delay is partly due to his camel's recent bout of dysentery. Yesterday it began in a mild form and now the animal is in a similar state to the one on the way to El Mudawwarah. Those days seem very far away. The other camels move well and have adapted to the daily distances, particularly now they are carrying less weight. The supplies of grain and water have been allowed to run down as we near Wadi Rumm, our final destination. I have resigned myself to being unable to ride onto Aqaba - it would not be possible to ignore the hospitality at Rumm following our return after a month; I am accustomed to their ways by now and know time means nothing to them, and the delay in stopping would be considerable. Even though it would complete the Lawrence routes to cover the final stretch to Aqaba, Wadi Rumm is somehow a more fitting climax to the venture - a rendezvous in the quiet privacy of a Bedouin camp. Aqaba with its many oil refineries, buildings, and holiday hotels is no longer the beautiful spot it was in 1917 and which Tom Beaumont had described.

As we wait, Mohammed begins teasing me about the pipe I smoke, drawing attention to his own particular lack of tobacco. After the incident at El Mureigha I am pleased to see him in high spirits, once more the main personality of the expedition and the instigator of much affectionate rapport. In four weeks he has smoked virtually our entire supply of cigarettes. His particular way of pleading for them, and the good-humoured glint forever in his eyes as he did this, normally ensured that either James or myself would take pity.

My father's old Kaywoodie pipe is obviously Mohammed's next acquisition in his craving for tobacco but I have no intention of it sharing the same fate as the binoculars. As I fill the pipe and hand it across I make this quite clear, telling him that contrary to Bedouin custom he may not keep it. Surprisingly he understands and treats it with great pride and respect because of my attachment to it. He laughs as he happily smokes, emulating the manner of an English gentleman. I am happy to share it with him. My father died eight years ago serving with the Gurkhas in Nepal.

The sandy passes between the sandstone hills channel us in a south-easterly direction. We are content once more in our monopoly of the desert, its beauty and its silence. The contrasts of rock colour, the sandy areas of fine red and yellow, the bright green shoots of plants encouraged by recent rain, and the shades of our own caravan are sadly indistinct without the sun. Nevertheless as evening approaches the sky begins to clear, and in four hours riding we have covered a good distance. I regret this progress. Now I no longer wish to see our journey's end. Mohammed smiles at my suggestions for camping sites and asks me mockingly whether it is I who is tired - I do not expect him to perceive my wish to play out the time for as long as possible.

'Bukra (tomorrow), Wadi Rumm,' he shouts as we ride together.

'Yimkin, Mohammed - in shaa Allah,' I reply, this time meaning these indecisive Arab expressions. He sucks on my pipe and grins, riding with the ease and fluidity of a master camel handler. Irrespective of our past conflicts and differences, I am reluctant to part from Mohammed and this tribal existence and return to conventional Army life: the entire venture has broken the routine of peace-time soldiering I find so unexciting. It has been a time to escape the responsibilities of Northern Ireland, the rank structure and chain of command, and above all the feeling that we are merely working hard for the sake of it. It has been an opportunity to be different, and to do something unorthodox and interesting compared with the insularity of Army life.

From the hills to our right an indistinct figure approaches at a run. His pace is urgent as if he aims to head us off, and I am a little mystified, as he comes closer, to make out a soldier in full battle order. Mohammed mentions something about a gun as he lowers the binoculars, and promptly dismounts. The soldier eventually arrives breathless, brandishing his American armalite rifle in a threatening manner and becoming even more edgy when he notices our European faces beneath the kaffiyahs. The initial encounter is not at all friendly as he questions Mohammed rapidly. We casually hand over our passes which he keenly scrutinizes. I notice his armalite has a round in the chamber ready for firing and that the safety catch is not applied. His finger is around the trigger and I feel a trifle unsafe watching him handle the weapon like a squash raquet, his authority dangerously mixed with cowboy bravado. I resist a temptation to step forward and apply the safety catch, and instead watch with amusement the bafflement on his face while he tries to work out who we are. I understand his unexpected appearance when I scan the nearby hills and pick out the positions of a further four soldiers at widespread intervals. The Army is obviously picketing the high ground as security for HRH Prince Charles and Princess Diana, who today are due to travel by road from Aqaba to Petra. Our route parallels that road a few miles away and the outposts will be to prevent terrorists infiltrating the desert to the east.

Although the soldier does not really know what to make of four bearded and sunburnt British soldiers standing before him with camels, I am impressed by the way he carries out his duty and, indeed, the efforts the Jordanians go to in ensuring the safety of the private Royal visit. With the point of his rifle he waves us on.

The light is fading when we reach the limestone rock which will be the site of our last night in the desert. The peculiarity of its mushroom shape reminds me of illustrations in school geography books, the base of the rock smoothed like the stalk and the overhang of the cap. It stands near the side of the pass like a landmark, a monument unlike any other to our final triumph; it will fix the evening in our memories for ever. The overhang is blackened by Bedouin fires of the past, each scar with its own story to tell - ours will only be another. There is an abundance of brushwood and the flames leap high as we enjoy, for once, piling it on extravagantly. Its light throws shadows within the hollows of the rock, an effect similar to holding a torch under someone's face on a dark night. Within the rock hollows there are faces too, alive and taunting us in the yellow light. Chris and Mark stand by the fire and I take a photograph which I hope captures the spirit of the scene before me - the outline of the couched camels, Chris and Mark in their thobes, and the rock behind, which seems to isolate them in the archives of time. We say little.

The stars are the most magnificent we have seen but there is no need for James to complete a fix of our position. Wadi Rumm is six hours ride away. It is the warmest night we have experienced and we feel fitter than ever before.

Our habits and actions are akin to the Bedouin's and we have become skilled riders of camels. Our integration is total and our wish now is to ride for Saudi Arabia and through the Hejaz mountains. No wonder, as he clearly recounted in the descriptions in *Seven Pillars*, Lawrence was deeply touched by his experiences. As I gaze into the flames it seems a contradiction for him also to have written: 'Pray God that men reading the story will not, for love of the glamour of strangeness, go out to prostitute themselves and their talents in serving another race.'

14 March

I wake to see a pale blue dawn with the moon still visible.

James emerges from his sleeping bag on the final day of the expedition.

Mohammed squats beside the fire he has just lit. He rubs his hands for warmth, hawks and spits the phlegm aside, wipes his face with the end of the kaffiyah, and places the blackened kettle at the side of the flames. I lie comfortably in my sleeping bag watching as he prods the fire with his camel stick and positions further kindling around the pot. Between a gap in the nearby hills the first rays of sun give the morning its colours. The camels remain couched, the deep gurgling noises from their stomachs are followed by the slow and continual chewing of regurgitated food. I study it all with the intensity of that first morning in Mohammed's tent - only this time it is not the novelty of the scene I retain in my mind but the knowledge that it is almost the last moment. I am full of regrets.

The sun rises quickly above the hills, one minute only a hint of warmth and the next a dazzling fireball. Soon the heat forces me out of my sleeping bag, the smell of which has become appalling - we sleep fully clothed, kaffiyahs over our heads as protection against the cold nights. The lice make their presence apparent very early and I feel uncomfortable, sticky and dirty, my body almost crying out to be cleansed as though sensing our proximity to civilisation.

After the normal breakfast of tea and bread, Mohammed and Hamad set to work on curing the last of our sick camels of dysentery. We are intrigued by their new method as Mohammed selects a number of rounded stones which he then heats in the fire. Chris's camel is forced shakily to its feet after considerable effort and much protest. Mohammed flicks the hot stones onto a rock slab and approaches the unsuspecting animal whose legs are securely hobbled together. While Hamad holds the head, Mohammed reaches under the camel and firmly presses the stones into its soft stomach. Between the animals screams of pain we can hear the flesh sizzling, and the smoke and smell of burnt hair and skin reaches where we sit. Clearly the intention is to force the stomach to contract. The scene reminds me very forcibly of the time near Jebel Ratyeh, our first experience of Bedouin First Aid, a time when everything was so new and strange. The worries and fears of those days seem far away now.

As we prepare to leave, a herd of camels with their young come down the slope to our front and head obliquely towards the pass. The sudden belchings and slobberings from Barmey echo all around, and we laugh at his first show of excitement for some time. Attracted by his mating call, a small brown nagar tentatively crosses towards our group, finally stopping short of Barmey and studying him with interest. I take a photograph as Barmey responds with a fine display of tongue, and the two of them stretch their necks out to sniff each other curiously. The entertainment is abruptly halted when the old man leading the herd strikes the nagar harshly. She bounds away to catch up with the rest of the herd, and Barmey bellows in annoyance.

When the herd is past we lead our camels off on foot (as we have always done for the first two hours of the day's travel), and Hamad walks beside me. With a smile he gestures me to turn around to see the old man scavenging our camp site and sifting through the fire like a hermit. I would have thought this natural for a desert nomad, and I begin to wonder whether Hamad attaches some status to the relative plenty of the expedition. The sand is hot under foot, and before long we are walking with the bottom of our thobes tucked up into the rope around our waists to increase the air-flow. The sun beats down from the clear blue sky, the heat reflected from rock and sand onto our small party wandering through this arid wasteland. Its ferocity is greater than at any other time, and quickly we develop raging thirsts. However, there is no water.

For reasons known to himself alone, Mohammed has emptied the containers. After a month of similarly irregular behaviour, I still cannot understand the Bedouin's lack of respect for water - it is utterly illogical and inconsistent with the accounts of desert travellers. We plod on wearily, experiencing discomfort due to heat for the first time since the Jafr plain - 20 miles remain to Wadi Rumm.

The scenery - rock formation, different sand colouring, shrubs, the shadows of the sun and the soft curves of sand dunes - is forever changing. The scent of the scrub is kicked up by the dust of the front camels, fragile and fragrant in their wake.

We gaze in awe at towering colonnades of rock that form a pass which leads to an expanse of golden desert. Riding as a group, the caravan descends a gentle ridge of sand towards a flat lake of buff-coloured mud. It stretches for half a mile each way, and the glare from the midday sun makes us squint as we search through the shimmering air on its surface to see beyond. It is ideal for a camel race, I decide, as I contemplate the scene - a small excuse for entertainment before the expedition is over and our camels are returned to their owners. The Bedouin agree, with good humour and a certain competitiveness. We check the loads and

153

manoeuvre the camels roughly into line with each other for the start. The hard mud is cracked into the million shapes of a jigsaw puzzle and the finish is selected as the tamarisk on the far side. A shout from Mohammed and the race begins, the camels breaking into a thundering gallop as we charge ahead in line abreast. The excitement mounts as the animals reach their full stretch and Hashan begins to ease gently into the lead.

'On, on, on and follow the hounds,' screams James in glee as he gallops past at a terrific pace, holding onto his head-cloth and bouncing precariously up and down in his saddle. I look behind - Barmey has stopped, Chris' camel never started, and Hamad gently trots at a more leisurely speed. The race is between James, myself and Mohammed who is a little to my right. Suddenly Hashan goes berserk. He plunges his neck downwards in his normal feint, jumps twice and turns so sharply I am nearly flung to one side by the velocity. After a desperate stampede for a few hundred yards, he turns again, increases his speed, and heads back to the start line. We are on a direct collision course with Barmey, and as on all these occasions I am totally out of control. I try to shout a warning but it only comes out in a gurgle as the impact of the saddle strikes me each time on the rise, forcing the air abruptly from my lungs. Mark ducks as we tear past miraculously missing him by inches and then screams, 'Ride him cowboy' at Hashan's fast receding rear. Only wishing I could, I grit my teeth and hang on tenaciously - knowing that a fall at this speed might be fatal. Hashan begins to buck wildly as he goes into an ever decreasing circle to the right, until finally the turn is so tight that he comes to a standstill. My loathing for camels peaks at this point and I hit him hard with my riding stick - it is a mistake. He halts again and this time heads me in Hamad's direction as I cling on once more. The strap of the camera bag breaks for a second time and my equipment crashes to the ground. My kaffiyah flies off, and my arms are numb from holding onto the front pommel. Hashan stops at the moment before impact with Hamad's camel and stands shaking his head from side to side, breathing loudly, with saliva running down his jaws. Hamad dismounts and soothes him encouragingly, but at this stage I am reconciled to Hashan's madness and decide that camel racing is out.

I look up to see that Mohammed is the first to reach the tamarisk. He tells me there is water ahead in the hills, an ancient Nabataean well used by the Bedouin of the area. We ride across the plain, flanked by imposing hills, looking forward to quenching our thirst. He leads us into the dark shadow of a re-entrant in a hill.

Here we gratefully dismount in the luxury of cool shade. My head throbs from squinting in the harsh light and wearily I sit down beside Hashan, only too happy to watch as Mohammed climbs the rock and disappears into a narrow cavern. He emerges with a bucket which he holds triumphantly above his head and allows the water to cascade onto the rocks below.

'Moya, moya (Water, water), Al Humdoolillah!' his voice echoes in the re-entrant as James carries two empty containers to him. The bucket is dropped by a long rope into the well which appears to be a natural one, the water accumulating as it runs off the hills, and Mohammed hauls it up several times before the containers are refilled. Hamad drinks for a long time before handing a full container to Chris. He declines until it has been boiled for our tea, fearing it might be infected and not wishing to go ill with dysentery after surviving this far.

James and I have no such scruples, and drink from the container. The water tastes earthy but looks clean except for one or two foreign bodies floating around. But when our thirst is quenched we begin to doubt the wisdom of following the Bedouin example, especially when Mark points out some goat's droppings and suggests a dead one might easily be floating in the well. (Later a medical examination was to prove I had contracted whip-worm - tracurus tracurum - in my intestine, which is caused by drinking water, and I suspect the Nabataean well on the Guweira plain was the cause.)

The scenery becomes increasingly dramatic and colourful in the mid-afternoon as we commence our final ride to Rumm. During the halt for tea I read Lawrence's description of his approach from the north, across the same tract of desert, and his words surpass any that I could find to capture its beauty.

'Day was still young as we rode between two great pikes of sandstone to the foot of a long, soft slope poured down from the domed hills in front of us. It was tamarisk-covered: the beginning of the Valley of Rumm, they said. We looked up on the left to a long wall of rock, sheering in like a thousand-foot wave towards the middle of the valley; whose other arc, to the right, was an opposing line of steep, red broken hills. We rode up the slope, crashing our way through the brittle undergrowth. As we went, the brushwood grouped itself into thickets whose massed leaves took on a stronger tint of green the purer for their contrasted setting in plots of open sand of a cheerful delicate pink. The ascent became gentle, till the valley was a confined tilted plain. The hills on the right grew taller and sharper, a fair counterpart of the other side which straightened itself to one massive rampart of redness. They drew together until only two miles divided them: and then, towering gradually till their parallel ramparts must have been a thousand feet above us, ran forward in an avenue for miles. They were not unbroken walls of rock, but were built sectionally, in crags like gigantic buildings, along the two sides of their street. Deep alleys, fifty feet across, divided the crags, whose plans were smoothed by the weather into huge apses and bays, and enriched with surface fretting and fracture, like design. Caverns high up on the precipice were round like windows: others near the foot gaped like doors. Dark stains ran down the

'Returning to Wadi Rumm: "this processional way greater than imagination", delighting in the perfection of Lawrence's words.'

shadowed front for hundreds of feet, like accidents of use. The cliffs were striated vertically, in their granular rock; whose main order stood on two hundred feet of broken stone deeper in colour and harder in texture. This plinth did not, like the sandstone, hang in folds like cloth; but chipped itself into loose courses of scree, horizontal as the footings of a wall. The crags were capped in nests of domes, less hotly red than the body of the hill; rather grey and shallow. They gave the finishing semblance of Byzantine architecture to this irresistible place: this processional way greater than imagination.'

To our tired but triumphant party the desert has lost none of its impact as described by Lawrence on 11 September, 1917. I ride slowly and comfortably, for Hashan has burnt off his excess energy, holding my copy of *Seven Pillars of Wisdom* open at this page and delighting in the perfection of Lawrence's words. It captures everything I see around me without flamboyance or unnecessary embellishment.

Mohammed rides at the front singing joyfully, and Hamad is beside me naming each and every hill known to him since childhood. Their excitement rises with every step taken whereas we become quiet and depressed realising these are our last moments in their company. The sheer-sided hills of the valley confine us like the walls of a tunnel, projecting us forward to the Howeitat settlement at Rumm and the climax to the expedition. There is no escape. As we reach the sandy ridges we sight the fort in the distance and know it is all over. My thoughts are of the 700 miles we have ridden in the steps of Lawrence of Arabia, and the reward of an adventure shared with the Bedouin, the profits of their company, the sharing of a simple and traditional life. These are the investments of memory for the future. It is impossible not to be deeply moved. I wonder sadly how much longer the Bedu will continue to survive as we have known them.

Mohammed whips his camel hard and gallops ahead through the tamarisk thickets until we lose sight of him in the dead ground. The remainder of us ride in single file, well-spaced, like a veteran desert patrol returning from a mission. We do not speak, neither do we ask each other's thoughts. The scene is too poignant and, in our own ways, we drink in this last flavour of the journey.

Earlier we estimated each man to have lost over a stone in weight, and there is no doubt we are hardened and robust from the rigours of this nomad existence.

We reach a small goat-hair tent surrounded by brushwood half a mile from the main settlement. Here Mohammed lies on cushions and rugs facing a fire with a young woman dressed in black beside him. Two half-naked children play in the sand and we are welcomed into this family as though always a part of it.

Chris and the author in Mohammed's tent.

'For the ordinary Arab the hearth was a university, about which their world passed and where they heard the best talk, the news of their tribe, its poems, histories, love tales, law suits and bargainings...' Seven Pillars of Wisdom

Being served coffee in Mohammed's small goat-hair tent, a mile from the main settlement of Rumm.

The woman we are told is Mohammed's second wife who must live in a tent provided by him but away from Rumm. There his proper wife still lives in the main family tent. Now I understand why Mohammed had galloped ahead of us two miles down the valley. I smile as he gently pats the hair of his small daughter who clambers all over him, pulling at his nose and grey beard, clinging with chubby fingers to his dirty brown robes. We relax with the family, happy for the moment not to be exposed to the remaining Bedu in Rumm - after our virtual isolation it will seem crowded by comparison, especially since we know we will not be moving on.

The woman fills a large bowl of water from the oil drum by the tent and sets it down between us. Mohammed drinks first before passing it to me. I raise it to my lips and delight in the sweet taste - until I spot the leech wriggling around at the bottom. To fish it out will be rude and I avoid any embarrassment by quickly passing the bowl to James. As he raises it to his mouth I whisper my find. He starts, drinks a little and passes it on to Chris and Mark. They politely follow suit and their small sips are in no way a reflection of their thirst - their eyes are fixed on the living contents of the bowl.

A Toyota pickup pulls up in a cloud of dust beside the tent, and Mohammed's son, Salem, jumps out. In the back are the four camel owners we know so well from the bartering at the police forts of Rumm and El Jafr. We rise and they greet us like long-lost friends, clapping our backs and shaking our hands enthusiastically. They examine their animals carefully and to my relief they seem content - not that it really matters anymore. As Salem loads the expedition baggage into the Toyota, I know this really is the end of our venture. We will ride the camels the last half mile to Mohammed's main tent but it will never be the same again. Another Toyota arrives and Abdulla comes to join us - his unwelcome presence perhaps the final nail in the coffin.

'Hashan ques (good)?' the wizened old man with the hooked nose asks.

'Awah, Hashan ques,' I reply and laugh. It would be a shame to disillusion him and when I look across at Hashan I realise I will miss him after all. It is the beginning of the goodbyes. The final parting from our Bedouin will be the most difficult. The prospect of a wash and a meal no longer hold any appeal. Somehow I do not wish to be cleansed of this, 'the inviolate house'.

Letters from home. 'When we came back we'd sleep on the floor, wouldn't eat three times a day. It was very difficult to adjust. I was very tranquil. Lawrence talks about this wretched routine...that just because it's midday our mind tells our body it's hungry.'

Aftermath

Mohammed Musa was arrested by the police on our arrival at Wadi Rumm. He was charged with not sharing the money for the camels with their owners. That night, around a blazing fire in the courtyard of the fort, James and I re-lived exactly the scene on 13 February, but we failed to decide whether Mohammed really had been a rogue or was innocent and had simply misinterpreted our original deal. Certainly he was cunning, but despite his exasperating moods he had guided us caringly throughout the expedition, and for that we admired and respected him.

We left Wadi Rumm by landrover the following morning. As we said farewell, Mohammed took my hand and kissing me on both cheeks twice he then held me at arms' length and gazed sadly through the tears in his eyes. Suddenly it was too much. I was caught with my guard down and had to walk quickly away, never trusting myself to look back as a spring of emotion rose up within me. I knew I had been deeply touched by Mohammed and the desert, and that I would always want to return.

Two months later, on 19 May, I stood by T E Lawrence's grave on the occasion of a special service to mark the fiftieth anniversary of his death. The weather was fine and I was surprised there were relatively few people at the small church of Moreton in Dorset. The moment was an appropriate one for reflection. The expedition had been a fitting commemorative gesture and had also brought me closer to understanding the man - closer than the armchair reader still struggling with that black and white picture.